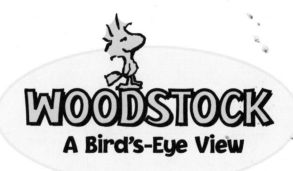

# WOODSTOCK

## A Bird's-Eye View

PEANUTS
!
flitter
flutter
flitter
flutter
flitter
flutter
whew!
GASP
GASP
4-4
Z
MUST HAVE
BEEN A
ROUGH FLIGHT
SCHULZ

PEANUTS
Tm. Reg. U. S. Pat. Off.—All rights reserved ©1967 by United Feature Syndicate, Inc.
GRIPE
GRIPE
GRIPE
GRIPE
COMPLAIN
COMPLAIN
COMPLAIN
COMPLAIN
COMPLAIN
4-5
CRAB CRAB
CRAB CRAB
CRAB CRAB
CRAB CRAB
IF HE DOESN'T LIKE IT, WHY DOES HE KEEP FLYING DOWN THERE EVERY YEAR?
SCHULZ

PEANUTS
flitter
flitter
flitter
4-6
I CAN'T FIGURE THAT GUY OUT...
HE'S EITHER A LOUSY FLYER OR HIS BLOOD SUGAR'S DOWN
SCHULZ

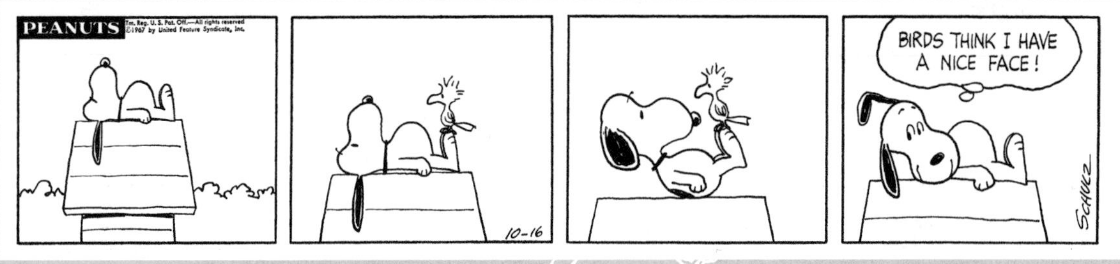
PEANUTS
Tm. Reg. U.S. Pat. Off.—All rights reserved ©1967 by United Feature Syndicate, Inc.
10-16
BIRDS THINK I HAVE A NICE FACE!
SCHULZ

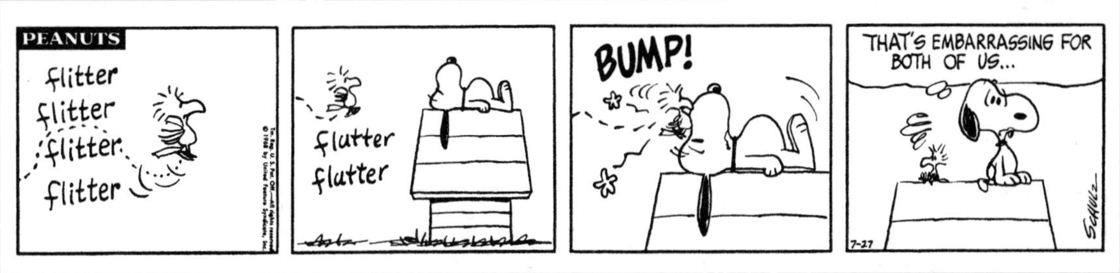
PEANUTS
flitter flitter flitter flitter
Tm. Reg. U.S. Pat. Off.—All rights reserved © 1968 by United Feature Syndicate, Inc.
flutter flutter
BUMP!
THAT'S EMBARRASSING FOR BOTH OF US...
7-27
SCHULZ

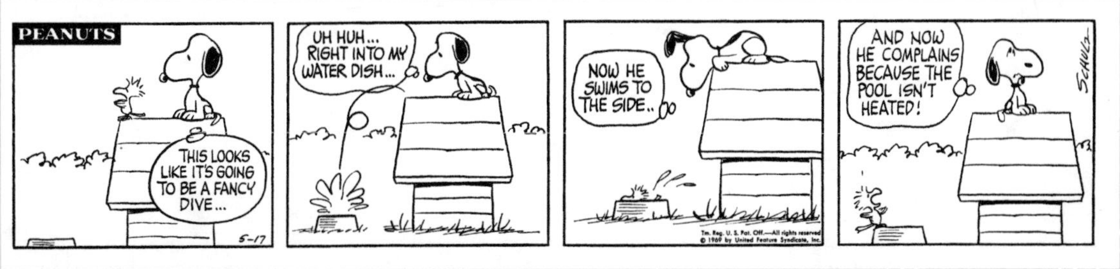
PEANUTS
THIS LOOKS LIKE IT'S GOING TO BE A FANCY DIVE...
5-17
UH HUH... RIGHT INTO MY WATER DISH...
NOW HE SWIMS TO THE SIDE..
Tm. Reg. U.S. Pat. Off.—All rights reserved © 1969 by United Feature Syndicate, Inc.
AND NOW HE COMPLAINS BECAUSE THE POOL ISN'T HEATED!
SCHULZ

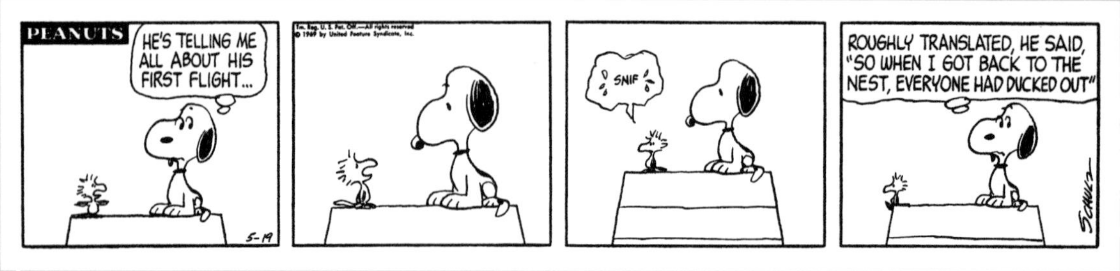
PEANUTS
HE'S TELLING ME ALL ABOUT HIS FIRST FLIGHT...
5-19
Tm. Reg. U. S. Pat. Off.—All rights reserved © 1969 by United Feature Syndicate, Inc.
SNIF
ROUGHLY TRANSLATED, HE SAID, "SO WHEN I GOT BACK TO THE NEST, EVERYONE HAD DUCKED OUT"
SCHULZ

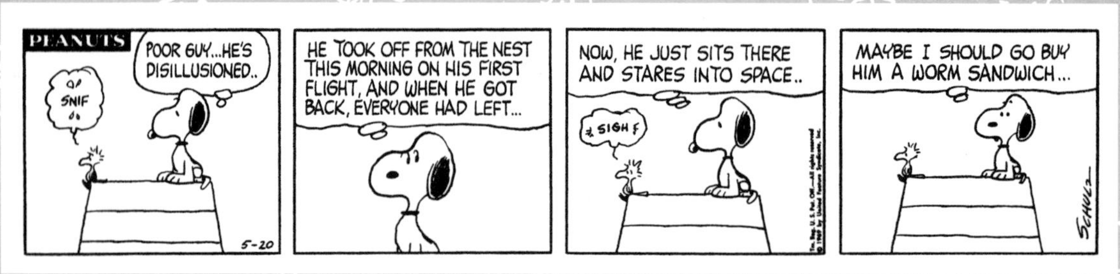
PEANUTS
SNIF
POOR GUY...HE'S DISILLUSIONED..
5-20
HE TOOK OFF FROM THE NEST THIS MORNING ON HIS FIRST FLIGHT, AND WHEN HE GOT BACK, EVERYONE HAD LEFT...
NOW, HE JUST SITS THERE AND STARES INTO SPACE..
SIGH
MAYBE I SHOULD GO BUY HIM A WORM SANDWICH...
SCHULZ

PEANUTS
Tm. Reg. U. S. Pat. Off.—All rights reserved
© 1969 by United Feature Syndicate, Inc.
12-9
PLOP!
SOMEONE IS SPOILING FOR A SNOWBALL FIGHT..
SCHULZ

PEANUTS
1-21
SLAP! SLAP! WAP!! SLAP! SLAP!
SOMETIMES I WISH HE'D GET HIS OWN BOTTLE OF COLOGNE
SCHULZ

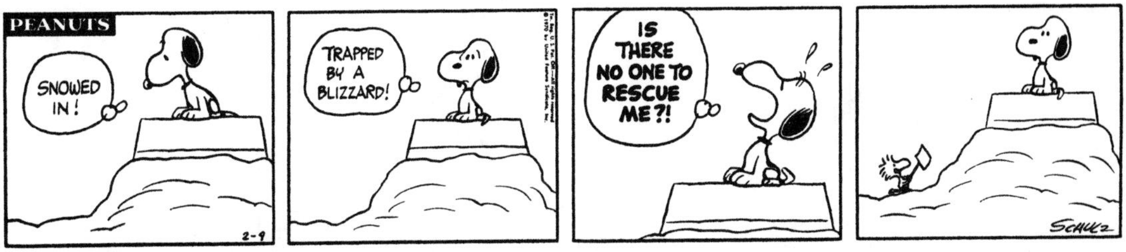
PEANUTS
SNOWED IN!
2-9
TRAPPED BY A BLIZZARD!
IS THERE NO ONE TO RESCUE ME?!
SCHULZ

PEANUTS
HE'S VERY GOOD WITH A SNOW SHOVEL..
I SHOULD BE OUT OF HERE BY THE FIRST OF AUGUST!

PEANUTS
I MUST SAY I ADMIRE HIS SPIRIT..
THERE'S ONLY ONE THING THAT BOTHERS ME...
WHO'S GOING TO RESCUE THE RESCUER?

PEANUTS
TUESDAY IS THE DAY THE HEAD BEAGLE HEARS CASES
AS SOON AS MY SECRETARY ARRIVES WITH MY LIST OF APPOINTMENTS, I CAN BEGIN..
BONK!
I MAY BE A LITTLE LATE FOR MY FIRST APPOINTMENT...

PEANUTS
Dear Sir,
2-26
THAT'S VERY NICE
PAT PAT
ALL SECRETARIES NEED A LITTLE COMPLIMENT NOW AND THEN..
Plx?g
SCHULZ

PEANUTS
NOW, THIS NEXT LIST WILL HAVE THE NAMES OF TEN MILLION DOGS..
2-28
I NEED A DETAILED REPORT ON EACH DOG'S ACTIVITIES TYPED UP IN TRIPLICATE
KLUNK!
I HATE IT WHEN MY SECRETARY FAINTS!
SCHULZ

PEANUTS
ONCE I WAS "HEAD BEAGLE"
NOW, I'M NOTHING!
3-10
AND MY POOR SECRETARY IS OUT OF A JOB
SIGH!
SCHULZ

**PEANUTS**

type type type

WRITING A BOOK, I SEE..

type type

PROBABLY HOPES IT WILL BE A BEST-SELLER ... THEY ALL DO...

type type type

WHAT'S THE TITLE?

" I WAS SECRETARY FOR THE HEAD BEAGLE "

SCHULZ

3-11

**PEANUTS**

type type type type

THAT STUPID BIRD IS WRITING A BOOK TELLING EVERYONE WHAT IT WAS LIKE WORKING FOR ME WHEN I WAS THE HEAD BEAGLE..

3-12

HEE HEE HEE HEE HEE

I'D SUE HIM, BUT ALL I'D PROBABLY GET WOULD BE A BUNCH OF BREAD CRUMBS!

SCHULZ

**PEANUTS**

MANUSCRIPT ALL FINISHED, EH ? READY TO BE MAILED TO A PUBLISHER, I SEE...

3-13

WELL, GOOD LUCK... LOOK OUT FOR THAT TREE!

BONK!

SO MUCH FOR THE MANUSCRIPT...

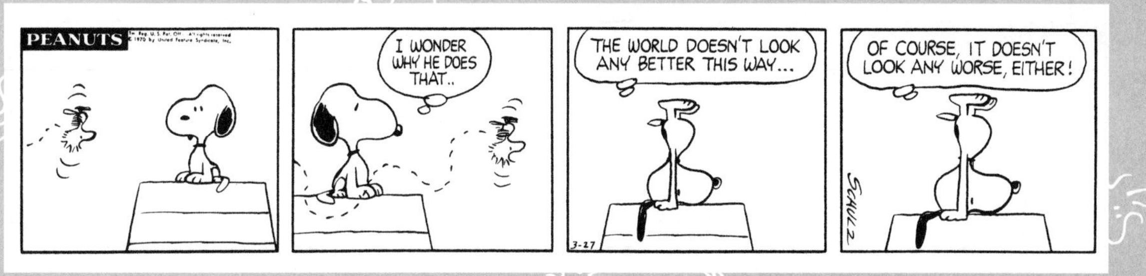
PEANUTS
I WONDER WHY HE DOES THAT..
THE WORLD DOESN'T LOOK ANY BETTER THIS WAY...
3-27
OF COURSE, IT DOESN'T LOOK ANY WORSE, EITHER!
SCHULZ

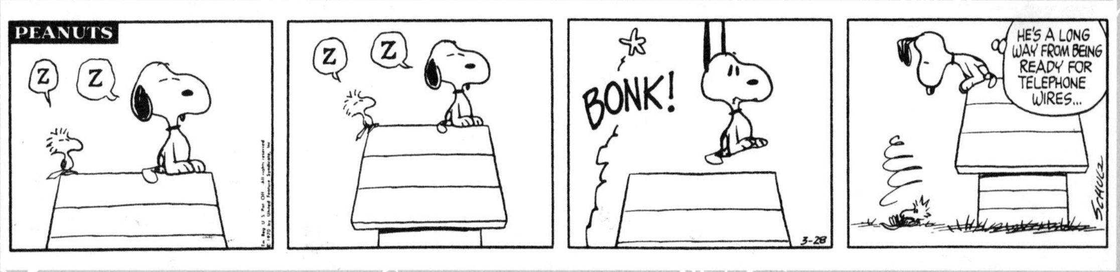
PEANUTS
Z
Z
Z
Z
BONK!
3-28
HE'S A LONG WAY FROM BEING READY FOR TELEPHONE WIRES...
SCHULZ

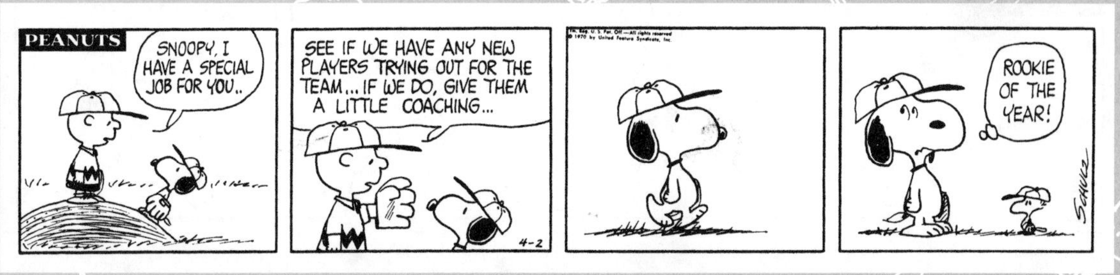
PEANUTS
SNOOPY, I HAVE A SPECIAL JOB FOR YOU..
SEE IF WE HAVE ANY NEW PLAYERS TRYING OUT FOR THE TEAM... IF WE DO, GIVE THEM A LITTLE COACHING...
4-2
ROOKIE OF THE YEAR!
SCHULZ

PEANUTS
BONK!
4-3
TWO HANDS!!
SCHULZ

PEANUTS
BEING A MANAGER IS A HARD JOB..
ONE OF THE MOST UNPLEASANT THINGS A MANAGER HAS TO DO IS TELL A NEW PLAYER THAT HE HASN'T MADE THE TEAM..
4-4
YOU NEVER KNOW HOW HE'S GOING TO TAKE THE NEWS...
BLEAH!
SCHULZ

PEANUTS
type
type
type
type
4-20
THIS IS NATIONAL SECRETARIES' WEEK
GIVE YOUR SECRETARY A HUG!
SCHULZ

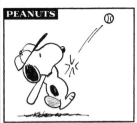

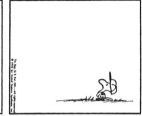

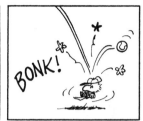

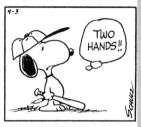

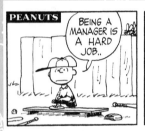

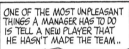

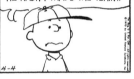

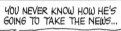

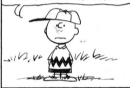

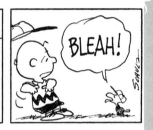

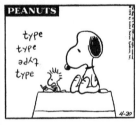

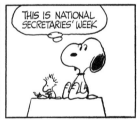

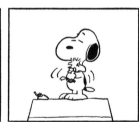

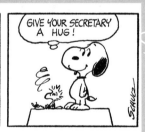

PEANUTS
THIS IS NATIONAL SECRETARIES' WEEK
A GOOD SECRETARY SHOULD HAVE A BASIC KNOWLEDGE OF ECONOMICS, BUSINESS ORGANIZATION, ACCOUNTING AND BUSINESS LAW...
A GOOD SECRETARY ALSO RETURNS PROMPTLY FROM SEED BREAK
4-21
SCHULZ

PEANUTS
!
?!
A COMMON SECRETARIAL COMPLAINT.. HE CAN'T READ HIS OWN SHORTHAND!
!
4-23
SCHULZ

PEANUTS
type type type type
type type type type type
HE'S NOT VERY GOOD AT MARGINS...
!
4-25
SCHULZ

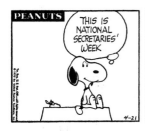

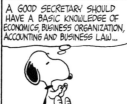

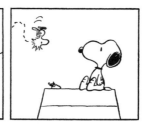

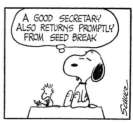

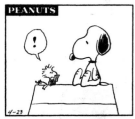

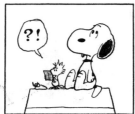

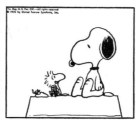

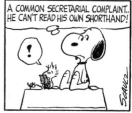

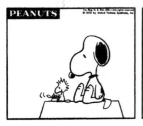

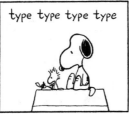

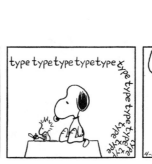

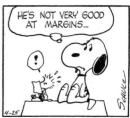

PEANUTS
Z
Z
I HATE PEOPLE WHO SING IN THE MORNING!
5-2
SCHULZ

8-8
© 1981 United Feature Syndicate, Inc.
SCHULZ

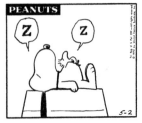

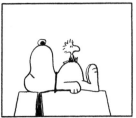

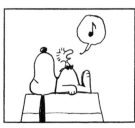

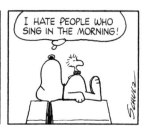

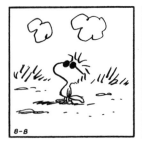

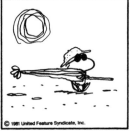

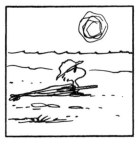

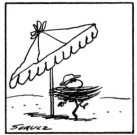

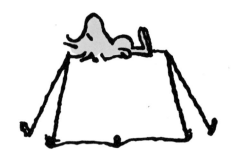

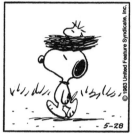

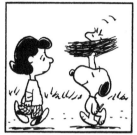

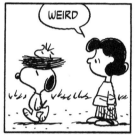

© 1983 United Feature Syndicate, Inc.
5-28
WEIRD
BUT POLITE
SCHULZ

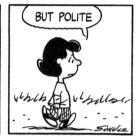

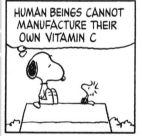

HUMAN BEINGS CANNOT MANUFACTURE THEIR OWN VITAMIN C
NEITHER CAN GUINEA PIGS, MONKEYS, AN INDIAN FRUIT FLY NOR THE BULBUL BIRD!
11-8
HAHAHAHA!
JUST THINKING ABOUT THAT MAKES ME FEEL GOOD!
HEE HEE HEE HEE HEE
© 1983 United Feature Syndicate, Inc.
SCHULZ

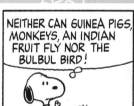

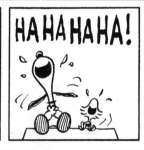

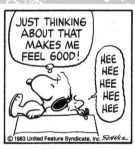

3-5
© 1984 United Feature Syndicate, Inc.
DON'T DO THAT!
I HATE IT WHEN SOMEONE COMES UP BEHIND YOU AND SAYS, "
SIGH
SCHULZ

YOU FOUND SOME GLASSES? THEY LOOK VERY NICE
SEE IF YOU CAN READ THIS CHART..
4-14
PERFECT!
© 1984 United Feature Syndicate, Inc.
SCHULZ

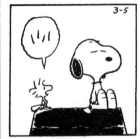

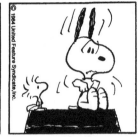

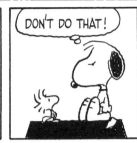

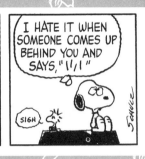

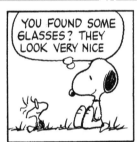

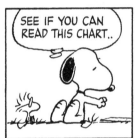

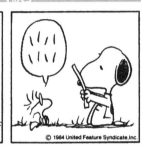

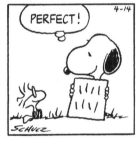

YOU'VE MOVED? WELL, HOW WILL I FIND MY WAY TO YOUR NEW NEST?
HERE, DRAW ME A MAP
4-17
NO, MAKE IT SIMPLER
YOU DON'T HAVE TO PUT IN ALL THE CONTINENTS..
© 1984 United Feature Syndicate, Inc.
SCHULZ

© 1984 United Feature Syndicate, Inc.
7-12
WELL, DON'T TRY TO WHISTLE IN THE WIND..
SCHULZ

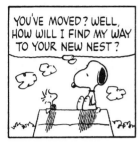

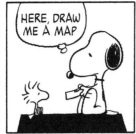

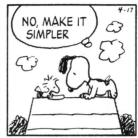

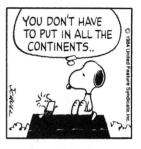

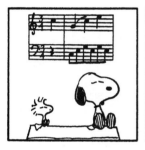

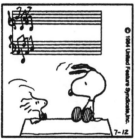

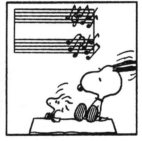

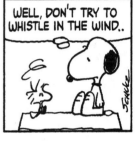

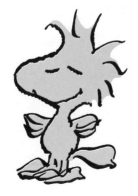

I USED TO WONDER WHY I HATED THE KICKOFF..NOW I KNOW
© 1984 United Feature Syndicate, Inc.
9-26
boot! boot! boot! boot! boot!
MY ARMS GET TIRED!
SCHULZ

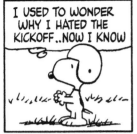

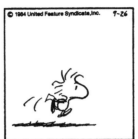

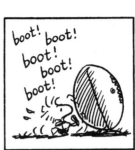

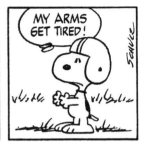

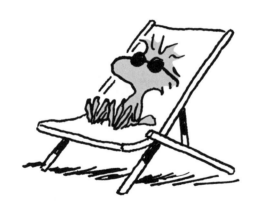

KIND OF
WINDY
TODAY
ISN'T IT?
© 1985 United Feature Syndicate, Inc.
3-25
SCHULZ

YOU SHOULD GET A JOB WORKING IN A TREE
YOU COULD BE A BRANCH MANAGER! HA HA HA HA!!!
© 1985 United Feature Syndicate, Inc.
3-30
SIGH
SCHULZ

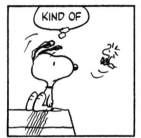

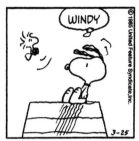

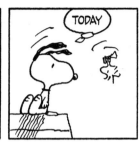

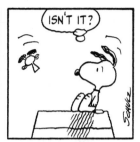

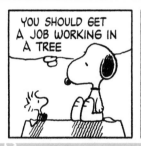

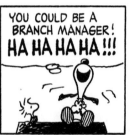

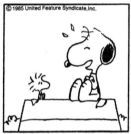

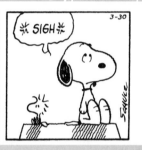

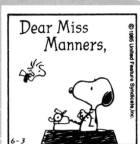

Dear Miss Manners,
© 1985 United Feature Syndicate,Inc.
6-3
Is it polite for a friend to sit on your nose?
Please excuse mY typpimg.
When he's Sitting th*re, i kant seee.

© 1985 United Feature Syndicate,Inc.
6-27
REALLY?
TELL ME MORE..
WOODSTOCK READS SUPPER DISHES!

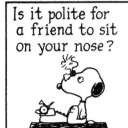

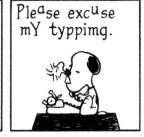

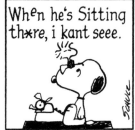

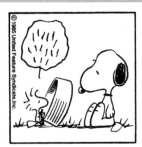

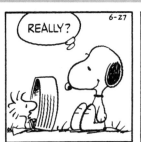

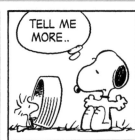

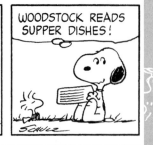

© 1985 United Feature Syndicate, Inc.
POOF!
YOU'RE WELCOME
SCHULZ
7-24

7-25
© 1985 United Feature Syndicate, Inc.
BONK!
SCHULZ

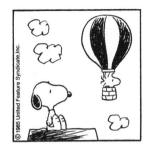

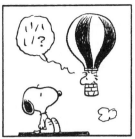

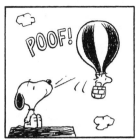

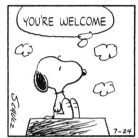

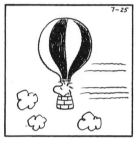

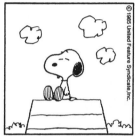

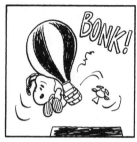

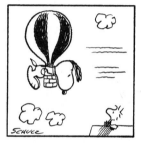

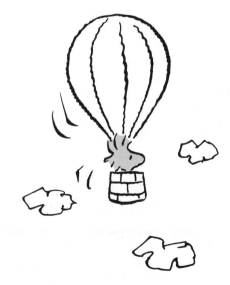

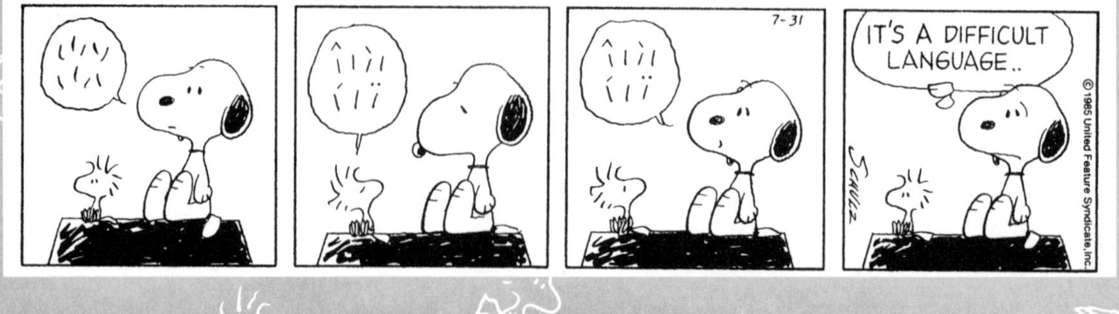
7-31
IT'S A DIFFICULT LANGUAGE..
© 1985 United Feature Syndicate, Inc.
SCHULZ

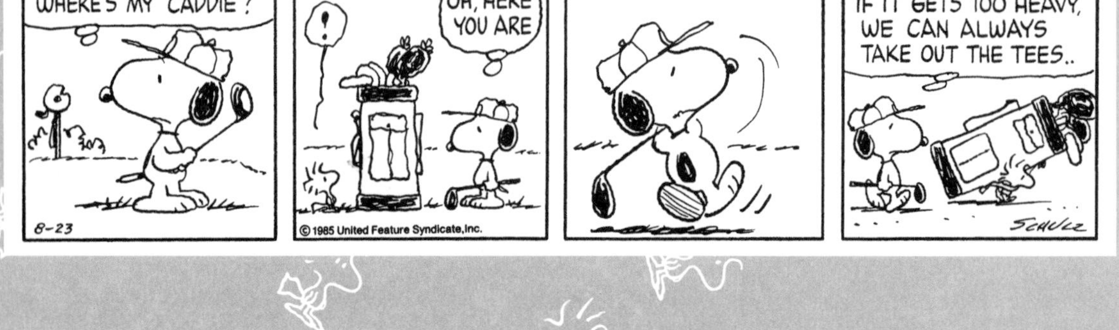
WHERE'S MY CADDIE?
8-23
!
OH, HERE YOU ARE
© 1985 United Feature Syndicate, Inc.
IF IT GETS TOO HEAVY, WE CAN ALWAYS TAKE OUT THE TEES..
SCHULZ

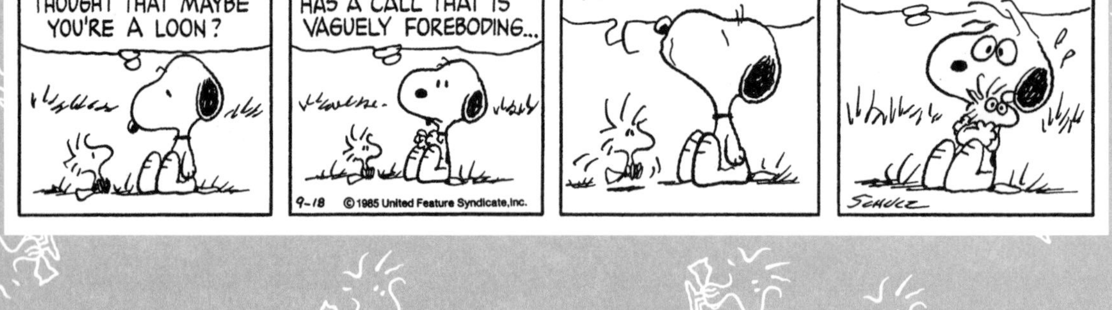
HAVE YOU EVER THOUGHT THAT MAYBE YOU'RE A LOON?
THEY SAY A LOON HAS A CALL THAT IS VAGUELY FOREBODING...
9-18
© 1985 United Feature Syndicate, Inc.
HA-OO-OO-OO...
TOO FOREBODING!
SCHULZ

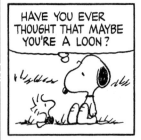

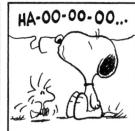

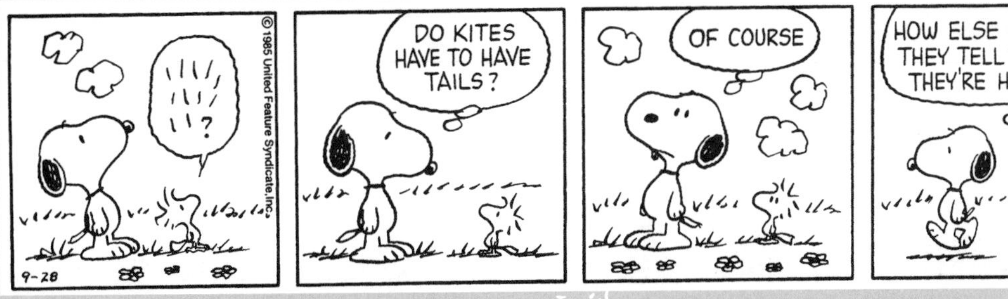
© 1985 United Feature Syndicate, Inc.
9-28
DO KITES HAVE TO HAVE TAILS?
OF COURSE
HOW ELSE COULD THEY TELL YOU WHEN THEY'RE HAPPY?
SCHULZ

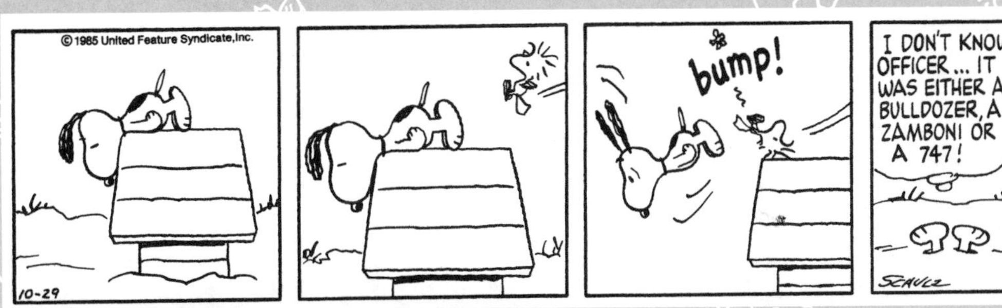
© 1985 United Feature Syndicate, Inc.
10-29
bump!
I DON'T KNOW, OFFICER... IT WAS EITHER A BULLDOZER, A ZAMBONI OR A 747!
SCHULZ

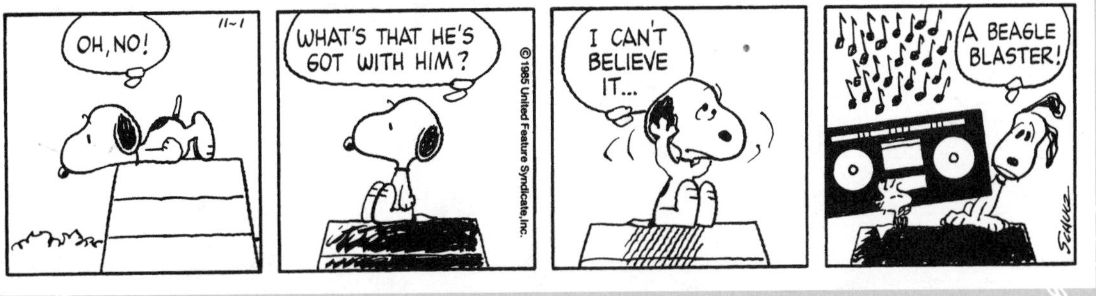
11-1
OH, NO!
WHAT'S THAT HE'S GOT WITH HIM?
© 1985 United Feature Syndicate, Inc.
I CAN'T BELIEVE IT...
A BEAGLE BLASTER!
SCHULZ

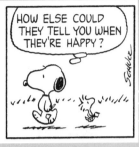

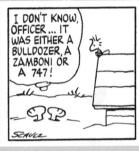

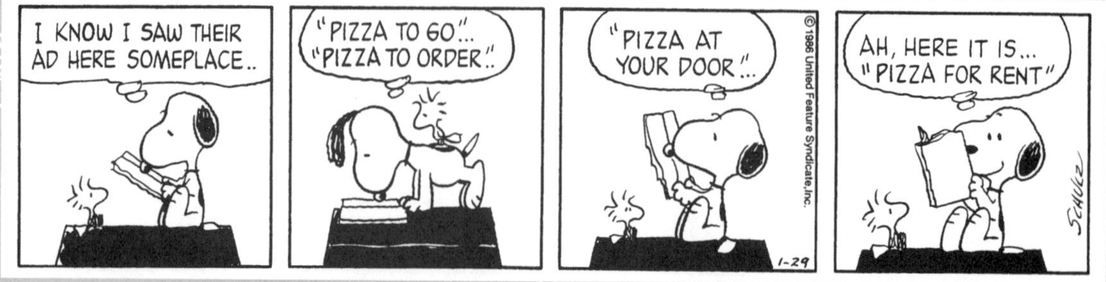
I KNOW I SAW THEIR AD HERE SOMEPLACE..
"PIZZA TO GO"... "PIZZA TO ORDER"..
"PIZZA AT YOUR DOOR"...
AH, HERE IT IS... "PIZZA FOR RENT"
© 1986 United Feature Syndicate,Inc.
1-29
SCHULZ

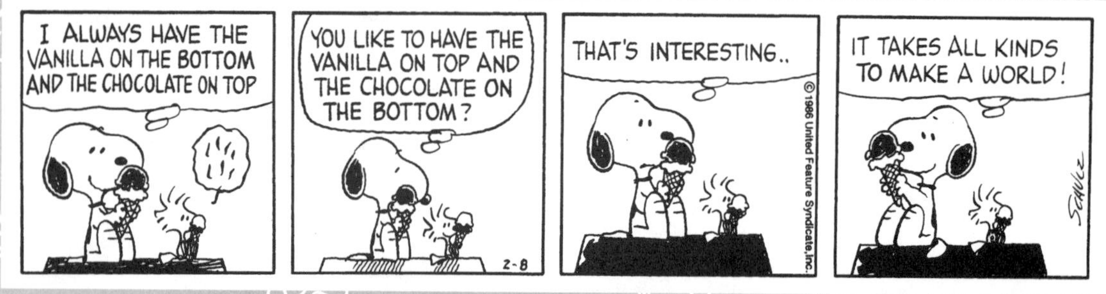
I ALWAYS HAVE THE VANILLA ON THE BOTTOM AND THE CHOCOLATE ON TOP
YOU LIKE TO HAVE THE VANILLA ON TOP AND THE CHOCOLATE ON THE BOTTOM?
THAT'S INTERESTING..
IT TAKES ALL KINDS TO MAKE A WORLD!
2-8
© 1986 United Feature Syndicate,Inc.
SCHULZ

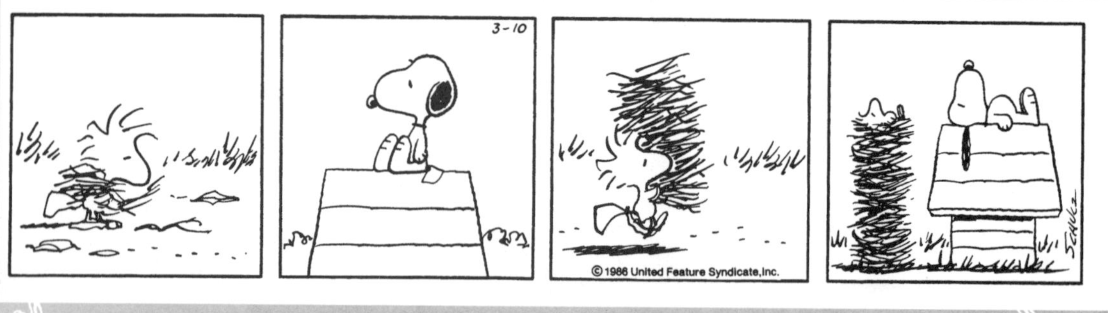
3-10
© 1986 United Feature Syndicate,Inc.
SCHULZ

OH, YEAH?
3-22
TAKE THAT!
© 1986 United Feature Syndicate, Inc.
WOODSTOCK HATES IT WHEN I PUNCH HOLES IN HIS ARGUMENT...
SCHULZ

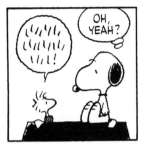

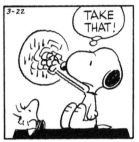

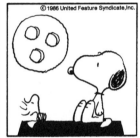

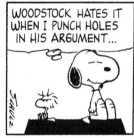

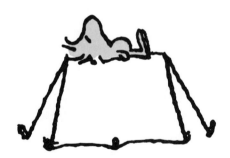

DON'T LOOK NOW, BUT SOME PEOPLE ARE WATCHING YOU..
I THINK THEY'RE BIRD WATCHERS...
4-7
© 1986 United Feature Syndicate, Inc.
HOW EMBARRASSING!
SCHULZ

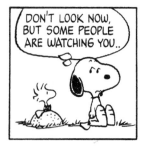

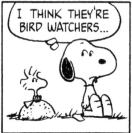

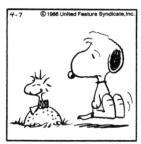

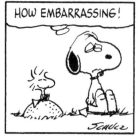

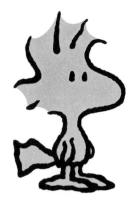

4-12
©1986 United Feature Syndicate,Inc.
SCHULZ

HE SAID HE HAD SOMETHING TO TELL ME..HERE HE COMES..
5-24
AND LOOK WHAT HE'S BRINGING WITH HIM..
NOW I KNOW IT'S GOING TO BE ONE OF HIS LONG STORIES..
©1986 United Feature Syndicate,Inc.
*SIGH*
SCHULZ

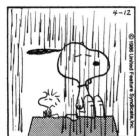

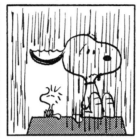

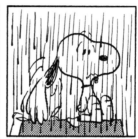

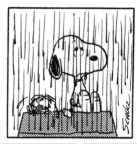

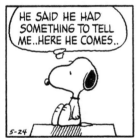

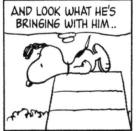

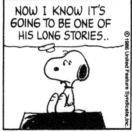

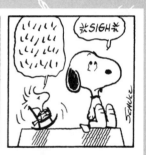

LONG HAIR IS OUT, YOU KNOW
SHORT HAIR IS IN..
© 1986 United Feature Syndicate,Inc. 6-21
ON THE OTHER HAND, MAYBE I WAS WRONG
SCHULZ

THE CRAWL? THAT LOOKS GOOD..
8-8
THE BACK STROKE? EXCELLENT!
THE DOG PADDLE?
NOW HE'S MAKING FUN OF ME!
SCHULZ
© 1986 United Feature Syndicate,Inc.

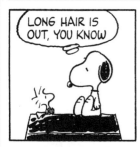

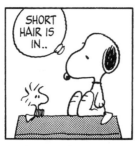

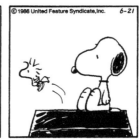

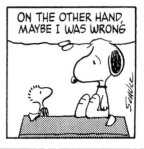

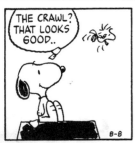

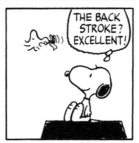

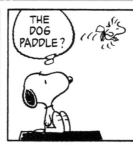

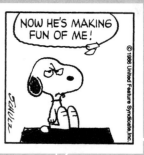

SEE THAT SQUIRREL? HE'S BEEN STORING UP FOOD FOR THE WINTER..

I'LL BET YOU NEVER THINK ABOUT THAT, DO YOU?

COME ON, TELL ME.. WHAT HAVE YOU DONE TO PREPARE FOR WINTER?

10-18  © 1986 United Feature Syndicate, Inc.

ONE THING THAT MAKES DOGS SUPERIOR IS OUR ABILITY TO RAISE OUR EARS..

LIKE THIS, SEE?

ANOTHER THING THAT MAKES DOGS SUPERIOR IS..

WAIT! I WAS GOING TO TELL YOU ABOUT OUR NATURAL HUMILITY..

12-6

© 1986 United Feature Syndicate, Inc.

31

12-11

EVERY TIME I LISTEN TO YOU, I'M REMINDED OF THAT OLD SAYING, "TALK IS *CHEEP!*"

HAHAHAHA!

© 1986 United Feature Syndicate, Inc.

EIGHT BALL IN THE CORNER? YOU'RE KIDDING..

12-15 © 1986 United Feature Syndicate, Inc.

HA! YOU MISSED!

NEVER PLAY POOL WITH A SORE LOSER!

32

1-1-87
YOU'RE GIVING ME A CALENDAR? HOW NICE..
© 1986 United Feature Syndicate, Inc.
I SEE IT HAS PICTURES OF BIRDS ON IT
LET ME GIVE YOU ONE OF MINE..
IT HAS PICTURES OF BEAGLES ON IT!
SCHULZ

YOU THREW AWAY THE CALENDAR I GAVE YOU!
IT HAS PICTURES OF BEAGLES ON EVERY PAGE! BEAGLES JUMPING OVER FENCES! BEAGLES RUNNING ACROSS FIELDS! BEAGLES WINNING "BEST-IN-SHOW"!
1-2-87
HOW COULD YOU DO SUCH A THING?!
SCHULZ
HE WANTED TO TRY OUT HIS NEW WASTEBASKET
© 1986 United Feature Syndicate, Inc.

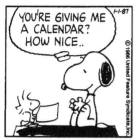

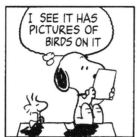

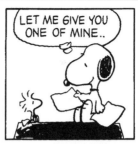

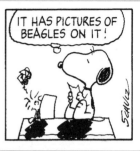

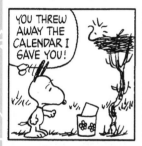

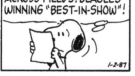

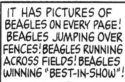

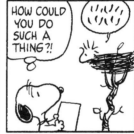

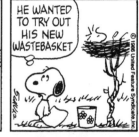

© 1987 United Feature Syndicate, Inc.
SCHULZ
4-13

6-26
© 1987 United Feature Syndicate, Inc.
FINE, THANK YOU
SCHULZ

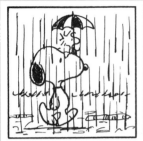

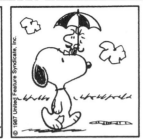

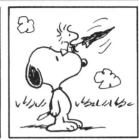

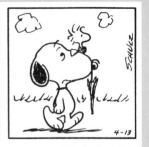

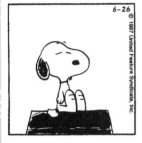

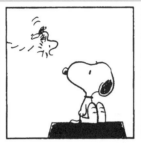

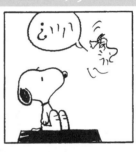

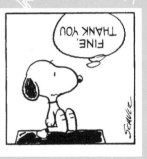

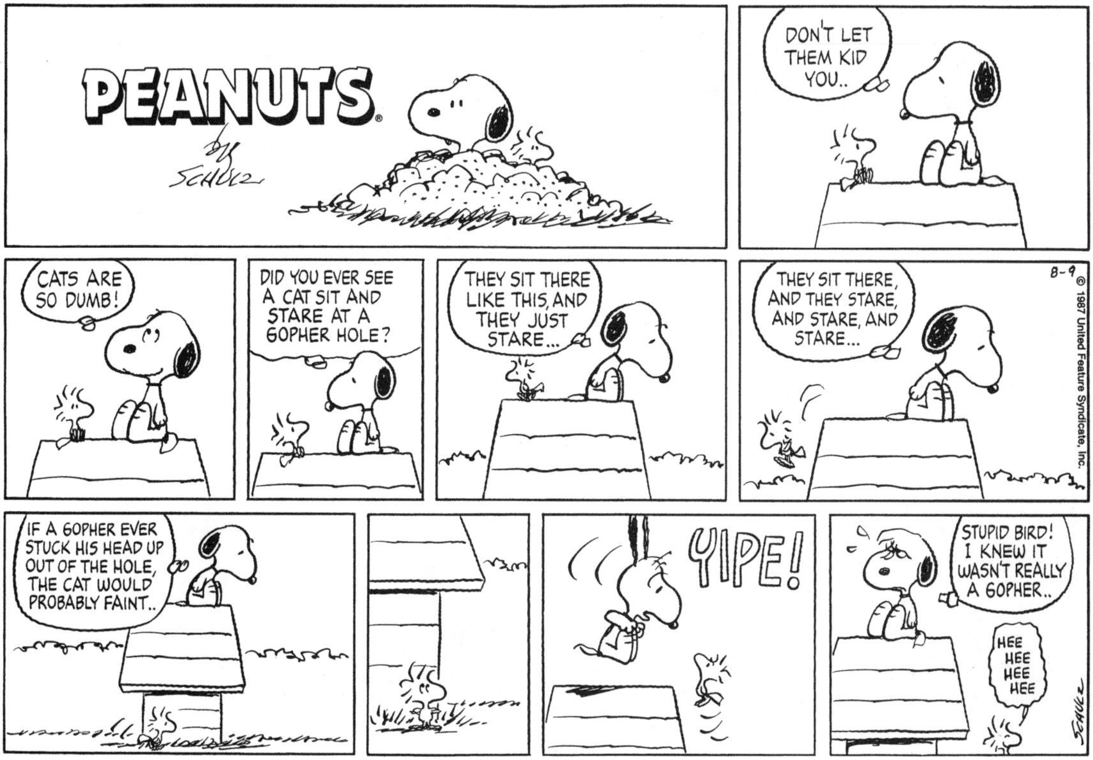
PEANUTS
by SCHULZ
DON'T LET THEM KID YOU..
CATS ARE SO DUMB!
DID YOU EVER SEE A CAT SIT AND STARE AT A GOPHER HOLE?
THEY SIT THERE LIKE THIS, AND THEY JUST STARE...
THEY SIT THERE, AND THEY STARE, AND STARE, AND STARE...
8-9 © 1987 United Feature Syndicate, Inc.
IF A GOPHER EVER STUCK HIS HEAD UP OUT OF THE HOLE, THE CAT WOULD PROBABLY FAINT..
YIPE!
STUPID BIRD! I KNEW IT WASN'T REALLY A GOPHER..
HEE HEE HEE HEE
SCHULZ

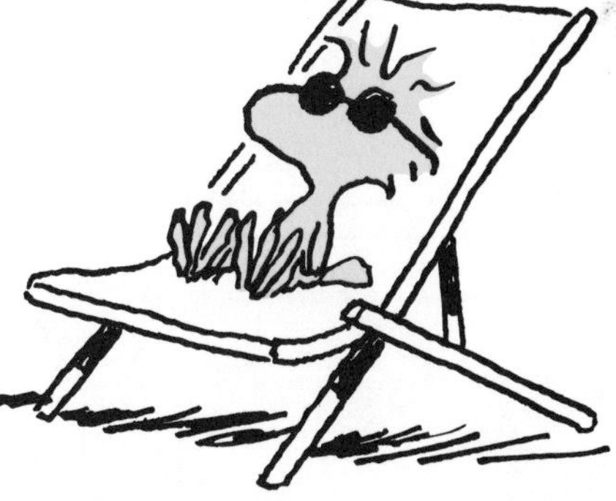

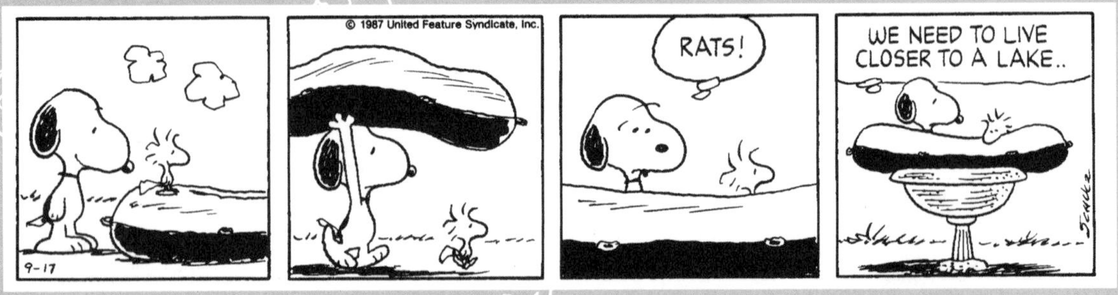
9-17
© 1987 United Feature Syndicate, Inc.
RATS!
WE NEED TO LIVE CLOSER TO A LAKE..
SCHULZ

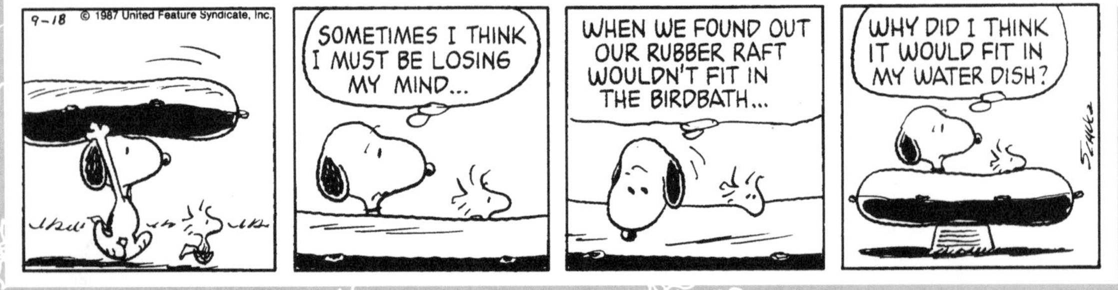
9-18 © 1987 United Feature Syndicate, Inc.
SOMETIMES I THINK I MUST BE LOSING MY MIND...
WHEN WE FOUND OUT OUR RUBBER RAFT WOULDN'T FIT IN THE BIRDBATH...
WHY DID I THINK IT WOULD FIT IN MY WATER DISH?
SCHULZ

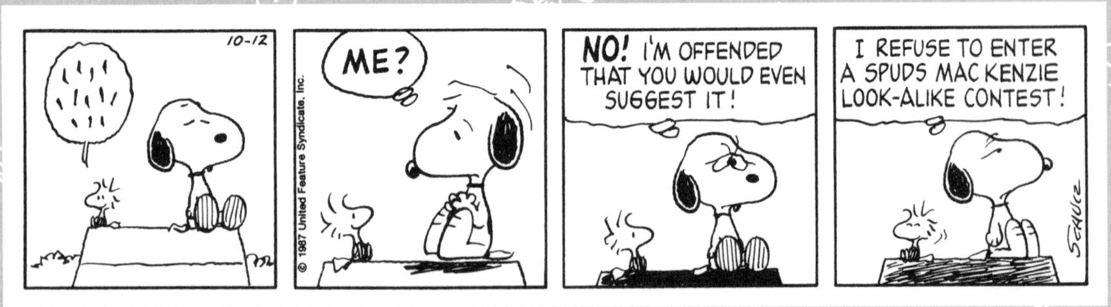
10-12
© 1987 United Feature Syndicate, Inc.
ME?
NO! I'M OFFENDED THAT YOU WOULD EVEN SUGGEST IT!
I REFUSE TO ENTER A SPUDS MAC KENZIE LOOK-ALIKE CONTEST!
SCHULZ

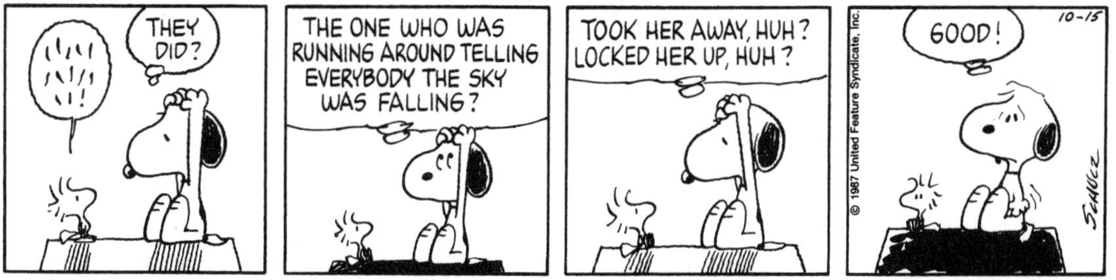
THEY DID?
THE ONE WHO WAS RUNNING AROUND TELLING EVERYBODY THE SKY WAS FALLING?
TOOK HER AWAY, HUH? LOCKED HER UP, HUH?
10-15
GOOD!
© 1987 United Feature Syndicate, Inc.
SCHULZ

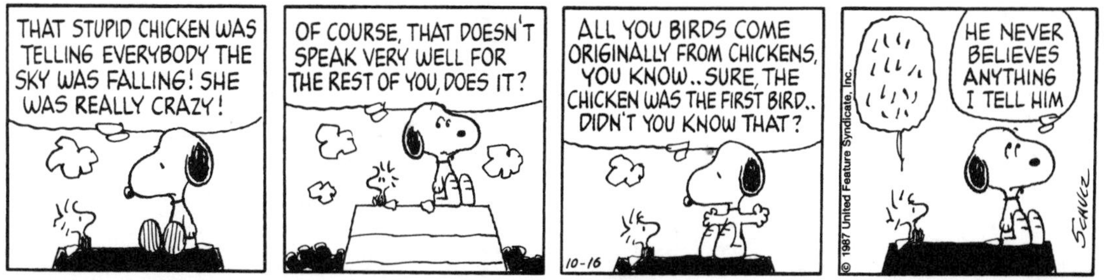
THAT STUPID CHICKEN WAS TELLING EVERYBODY THE SKY WAS FALLING! SHE WAS REALLY CRAZY!
OF COURSE, THAT DOESN'T SPEAK VERY WELL FOR THE REST OF YOU, DOES IT?
ALL YOU BIRDS COME ORIGINALLY FROM CHICKENS, YOU KNOW.. SURE, THE CHICKEN WAS THE FIRST BIRD.. DIDN'T YOU KNOW THAT?
10-16
© 1987 United Feature Syndicate, Inc.
HE NEVER BELIEVES ANYTHING I TELL HIM
SCHULZ

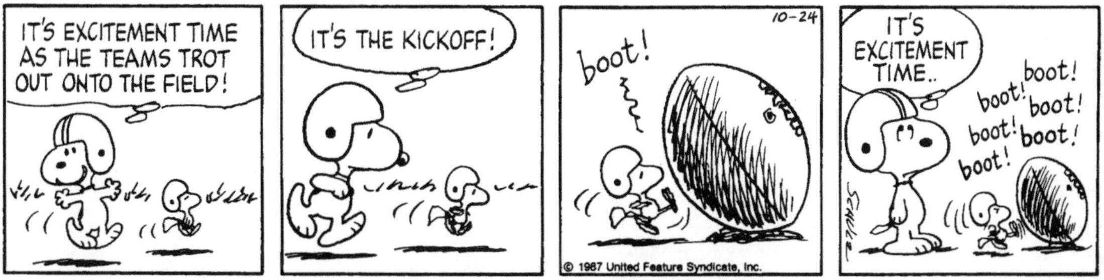
IT'S EXCITEMENT TIME AS THE TEAMS TROT OUT ONTO THE FIELD!
IT'S THE KICKOFF!
10-24
boot!
© 1987 United Feature Syndicate, Inc.
IT'S EXCITEMENT TIME..
boot! boot! boot! boot! boot! boot!
SCHULZ

WELL, DO YOU HAVE ANY PLANS FOR THE NEW YEAR?
1-1-88
JUST GONNA KEEP CHIRPING AWAY, HUH?
SCHULZ
© 1987 United Feature Syndicate, Inc.

NO, NOT REALLY
1-19
THE ONES WHO WENT WERE VOLUNTEERS..
SO YOU DON'T HAVE TO GO TO THE MOON IF YOU DON'T WANT TO..
WHEW!
SCHULZ
© 1988 United Feature Syndicate, Inc.

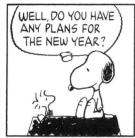

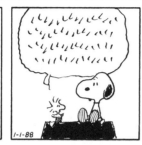

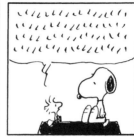

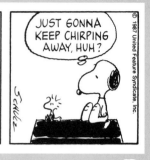

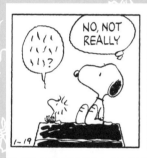

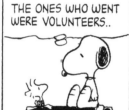

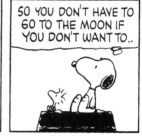

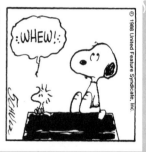

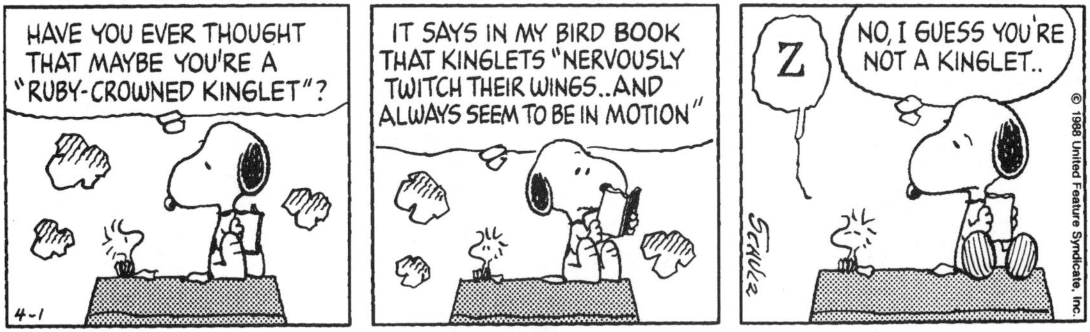
HAVE YOU EVER THOUGHT THAT MAYBE YOU'RE A "RUBY-CROWNED KINGLET"?
4-1
IT SAYS IN MY BIRD BOOK THAT KINGLETS "NERVOUSLY TWITCH THEIR WINGS..AND ALWAYS SEEM TO BE IN MOTION"
Z
NO, I GUESS YOU'RE NOT A KINGLET..
SCHULZ
© 1988 United Feature Syndicate, Inc.

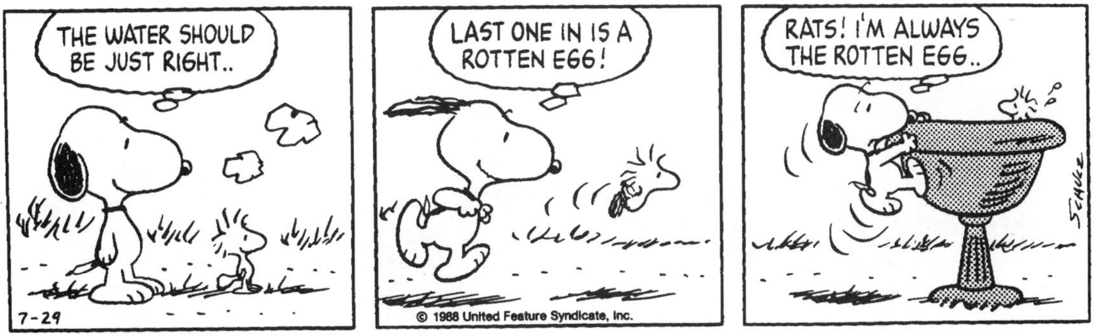
THE WATER SHOULD BE JUST RIGHT..
7-29
LAST ONE IN IS A ROTTEN EGG!
© 1988 United Feature Syndicate, Inc.
RATS! I'M ALWAYS THE ROTTEN EGG..
SCHULZ

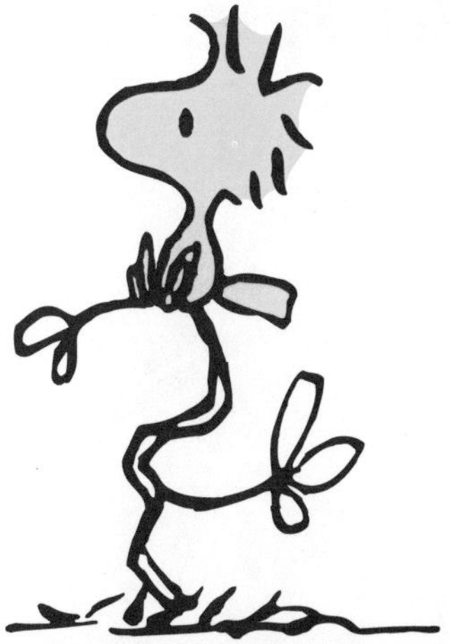

YOU'RE LUCKY YOU CAN FLY.. IF I WERE YOU, I'D FLY CLEAR AROUND THE WORLD!
© 1988 United Feature Syndicate, Inc.
?
10-8
WELL, NO.. NOT IF YOU HATE TRAVELING..
SCHULZ

ANOTHER REJECTION SLIP... FILE IT WITH THE OTHERS!
© 1988 United Feature Syndicate, Inc.
10-22
I'M NOT SURE I'D WANT TO SEE HIS FILING SYSTEM..
SCHULZ

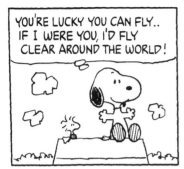

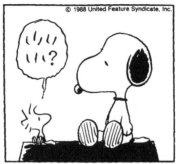

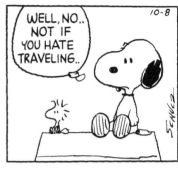

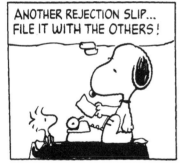

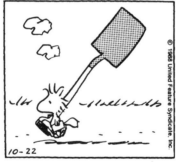

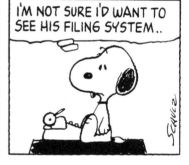

IT WAS COLD LAST NIGHT...
I'LL BET ANYTHING MY
WATER DISH IS FROZEN..
© 1988 United Feature Syndicate, Inc.
11-10
I
WAS
RIGHT..
I COULD
HEAR
WOODSTOCK
DRIVING THE
ZAMBONI..

ZAMBONI
DRIVERS
ARE VERY
SENSITIVE
© 1988 United Feature Syndicate, Inc.
11-12
THEY GET
QUITE UPSET
WHEN THEY
FALL THROUGH
THE ICE!
!
SCHULZ

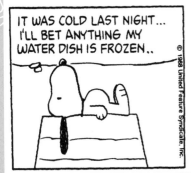

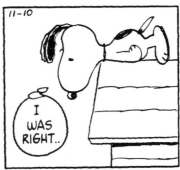

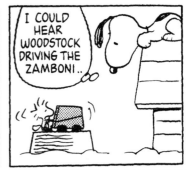

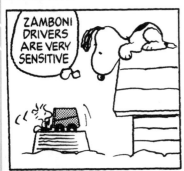

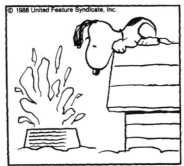

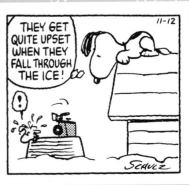

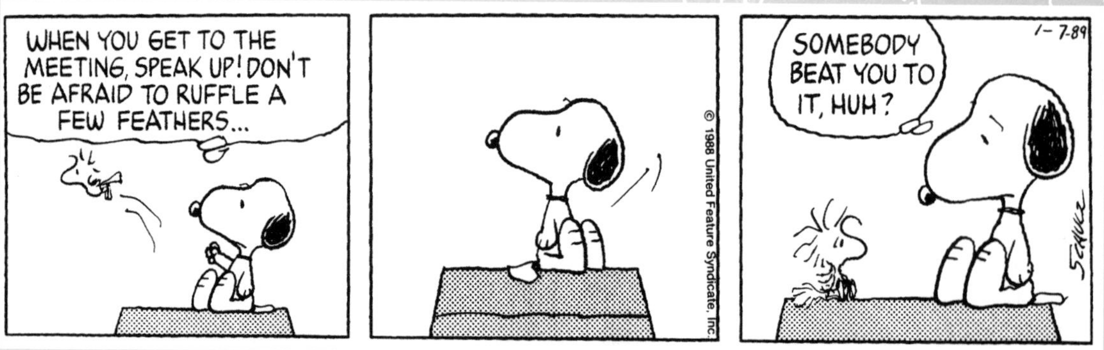
WHEN YOU GET TO THE MEETING, SPEAK UP! DON'T BE AFRAID TO RUFFLE A FEW FEATHERS...
© 1988 United Feature Syndicate, Inc.
1-7-89
SOMEBODY BEAT YOU TO IT, HUH?
SCHULZ

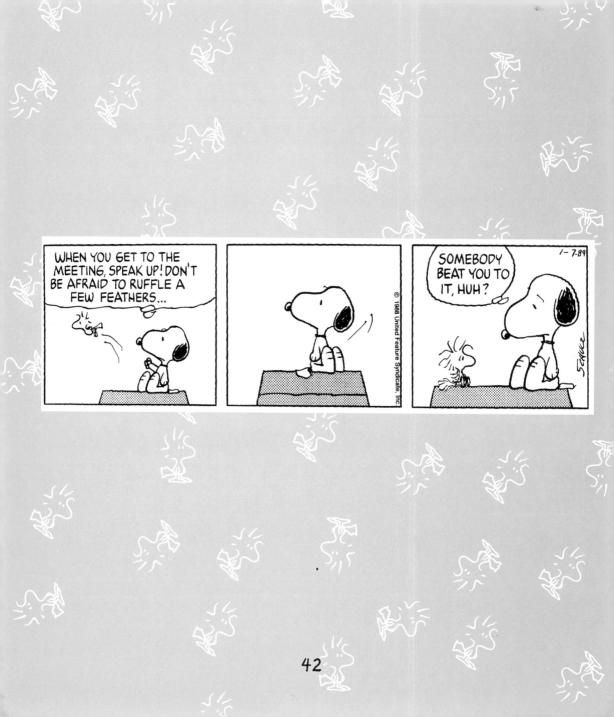

2-23
WOODSTOCK'S TINY LITTLE SNOWMEN ARE KIND OF CUTE..
© 1989 United Feature Syndicate, Inc.
SCHULZ
BUT I DON'T THINK HIS TINY LITTLE SNOWDOGS ARE CUTE AT ALL!

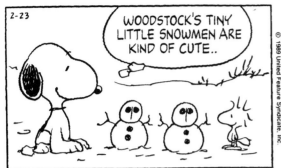

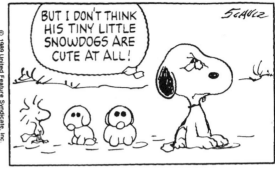

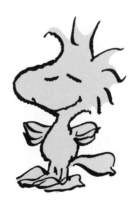

9-11
I HEAR A STRANGE ROARING IN THE DISTANCE.. WE'D BETTER PADDLE LIKE MAD!
© 1989 United Feature Syndicate, Inc.
SCHULZ

9-13
NO, YOU NEVER MENTIONED A WORD ABOUT PORTAGING..
© 1989 United Feature Syndicate, Inc.
SCHULZ

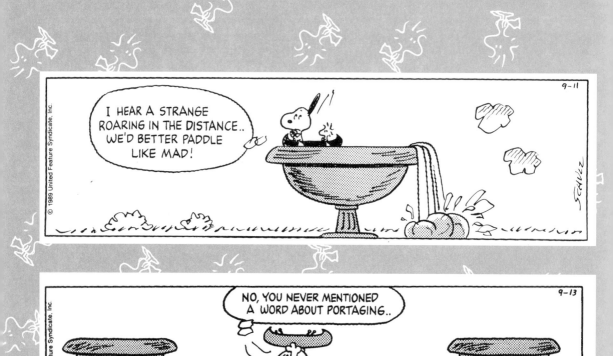

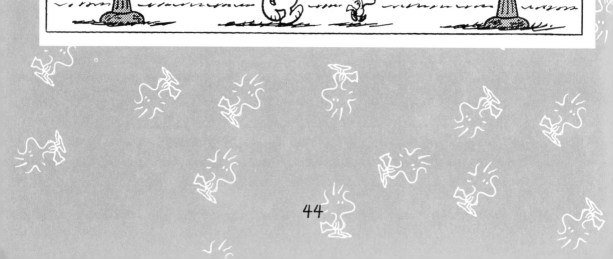

YOU'RE SUPPOSED TO SHOUT, "LAND, HO!"
..NOT, "EDGE OF THE BIRDBATH, HO!"
© 1989 United Feature Syndicate, Inc.
9-15
SCHULZ

I'VE BEEN CARSICK AND I'VE BEEN AIRSICK...
BUT THIS IS THE FIRST TIME I'VE EVER BEEN "BIRDBATH SICK"!
© 1989 United Feature Syndicate, Inc.
SCHULZ
9-16

© 1989 United Feature Syndicate, Inc.
11-28
SCHULZ

12-2
© 1989 United Feature Syndicate, Inc.
?
NO, I WAS WAITING FOR YOU TO MOVE
SCHULZ

1-9
© 1990 United Feature Syndicate, Inc.
SCHULZ

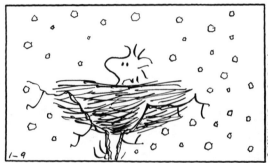

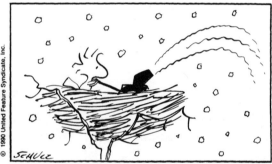

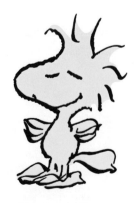

NO, YOU CAN'T BE A SHEPHERD BECAUSE YOU DON'T HAVE ANY SHEEP..
© 1990 United Feature Syndicate, Inc.
1-20
?
BAA!
I MUST BE OUT OF MY MIND..
SCHULZ

?
SURE, WHY NOT?
1-22
© 1990 United Feature Syndicate, Inc.
WELL, PUT IT ON, AND LET ME SEE...
YES, IT DOES MAKE YOU LOOK TALLER
SCHULZ

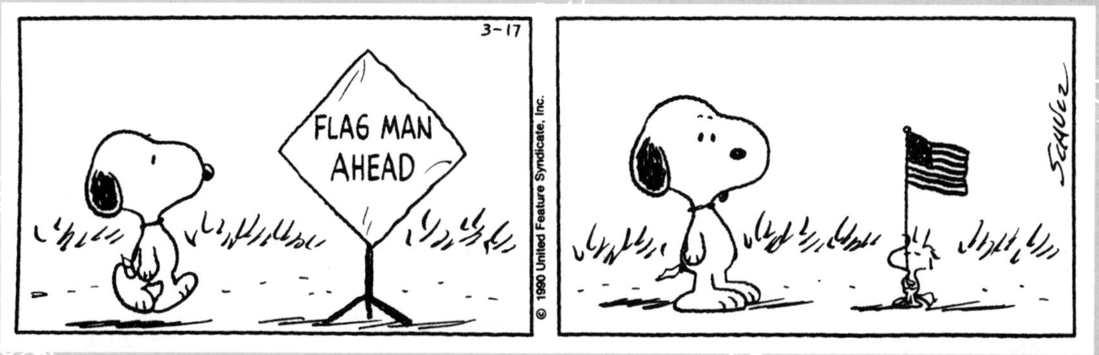
3-17
FLAG MAN AHEAD
© 1990 United Feature Syndicate, Inc.
SCHULZ

3-26
THAT'S RIGHT.. IT'S YOUR JOB TO TELL EVERYONE THAT SPRING HAS COME..
© 1990 United Feature Syndicate, Inc.
BUT NOT IN DETAIL!
SCHULZ

HERE'S THE WORLD FAMOUS NATURALIST GOING OUT ON A BIRD-COUNTING WALK...
© 1990 United Feature Syndicate, Inc.
5-28
THERE'S ONE!!
WOODSTOCK HATES BIRD-COUNTING JOKES..
!
SCHULZ

6-18
© 1990 United Feature Syndicate, Inc.
BUMP
?!!
NO, MY TURN SIGNAL IS NOT BROKEN!
SCHULZ

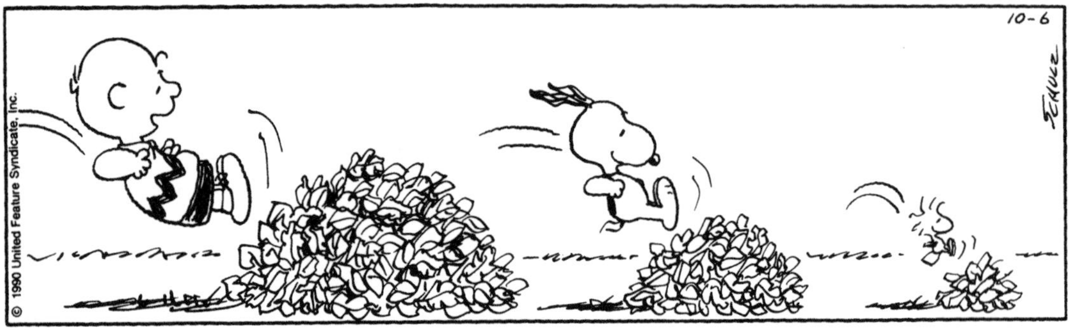
10-6
SCHULZ
© 1990 United Feature Syndicate, Inc.

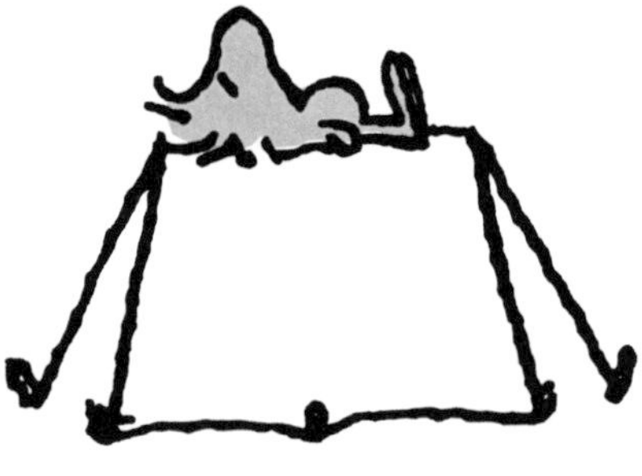

10-30
© 1990 United Feature Syndicate, Inc.
I GUESS SO..
BUT THERE'S MORE TO LIFE THAN BEING CUTE..
SCHULZ

© 1990 United Feature Syndicate, Inc.
ANOTHER ONE OF THOSE WHO DOESN'T TAKE THE GROCERY CART BACK..
11-6
SCHULZ

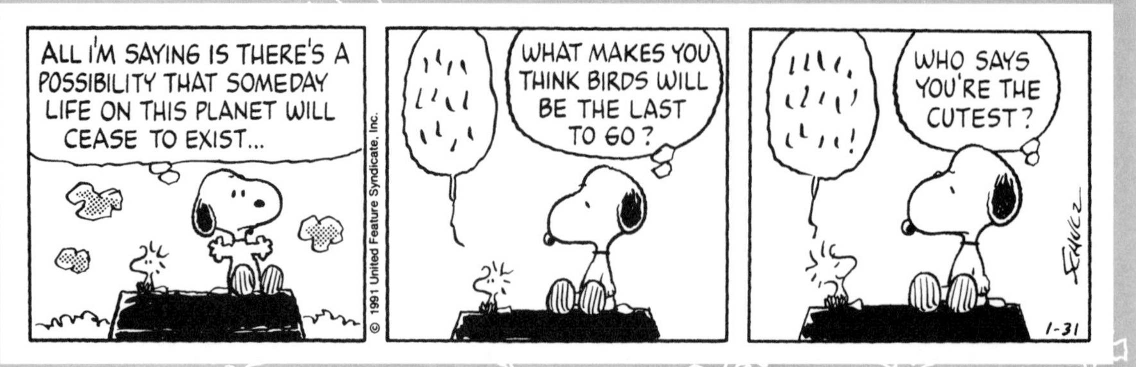
ALL I'M SAYING IS THERE'S A POSSIBILITY THAT SOMEDAY LIFE ON THIS PLANET WILL CEASE TO EXIST...
© 1991 United Feature Syndicate, Inc.
WHAT MAKES YOU THINK BIRDS WILL BE THE LAST TO GO?
WHO SAYS YOU'RE THE CUTEST?
SCHULZ
1-31

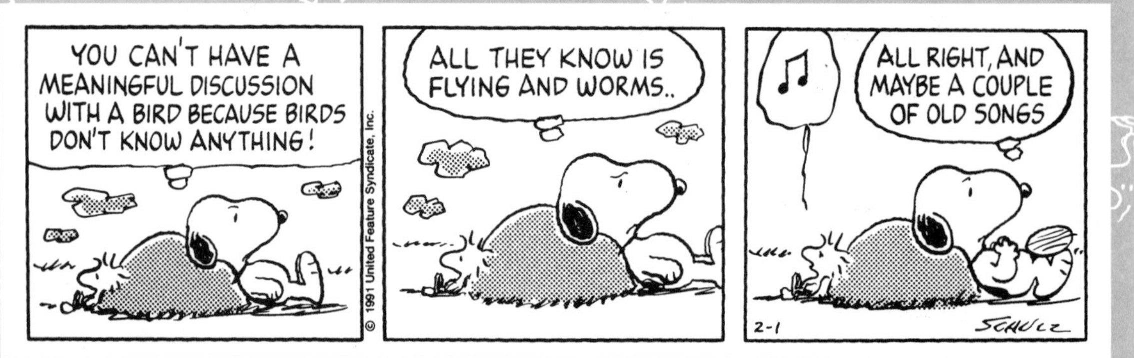
YOU CAN'T HAVE A MEANINGFUL DISCUSSION WITH A BIRD BECAUSE BIRDS DON'T KNOW ANYTHING!
© 1991 United Feature Syndicate, Inc.
ALL THEY KNOW IS FLYING AND WORMS..
ALL RIGHT, AND MAYBE A COUPLE OF OLD SONGS
2-1
SCHULZ

11-2
© 1991 United Feature Syndicate, Inc.
SORRY, THE PUNCH LINE WENT RIGHT OVER MY HEAD!
SCHULZ

ANYBODY HOME?
NO, I REALIZE YOU'RE NOT JUST ANYBODY..
5-20
SCHULZ
© 1992 United Feature Syndicate, Inc.

IT'S A KNOWN FACT THAT DOGS ARE MORE ATHLETIC THAN BIRDS..
© 1992 United Feature Syndicate, Inc.
5-23
MOST BIRDS
SCHULZ

9-16
YOU LIKE SPRING BETTER THAN FALL?
© 1992 United Feature Syndicate, Inc.
WELL, YES... I CAN UNDERSTAND THAT..
SCHULZ

SEE THAT SKY? THAT SKY IS YOURS!
YOU'RE A BIRD! SOAR AS HIGH AS YOU WANT!
© 1992 United Feature Syndicate, Inc.
YOU CAN OWN THE SKY..
SORT OF..
SCHULZ
11-12

THE WORLD IS YOURS.. A SKY TO FLY IN...
AND A GROUND FILLED WITH MILLIONS OF WORMS!
© 1992 United Feature Syndicate, Inc.
SCHULZ
11-13

THANKSGIVING IS OVER!

11-26

© 1992 United Feature Syndicate, Inc.

WELL, I IMAGINE THE REASON YOU CAN'T THROW A SNOWBALL IS YOU DON'T HAVE ANY HANDS..

OF COURSE, YOU COULD ALWAYS JUST "WING" IT!

© 1993 United Feature Syndicate, Inc.

HA HA HA HA

2-24

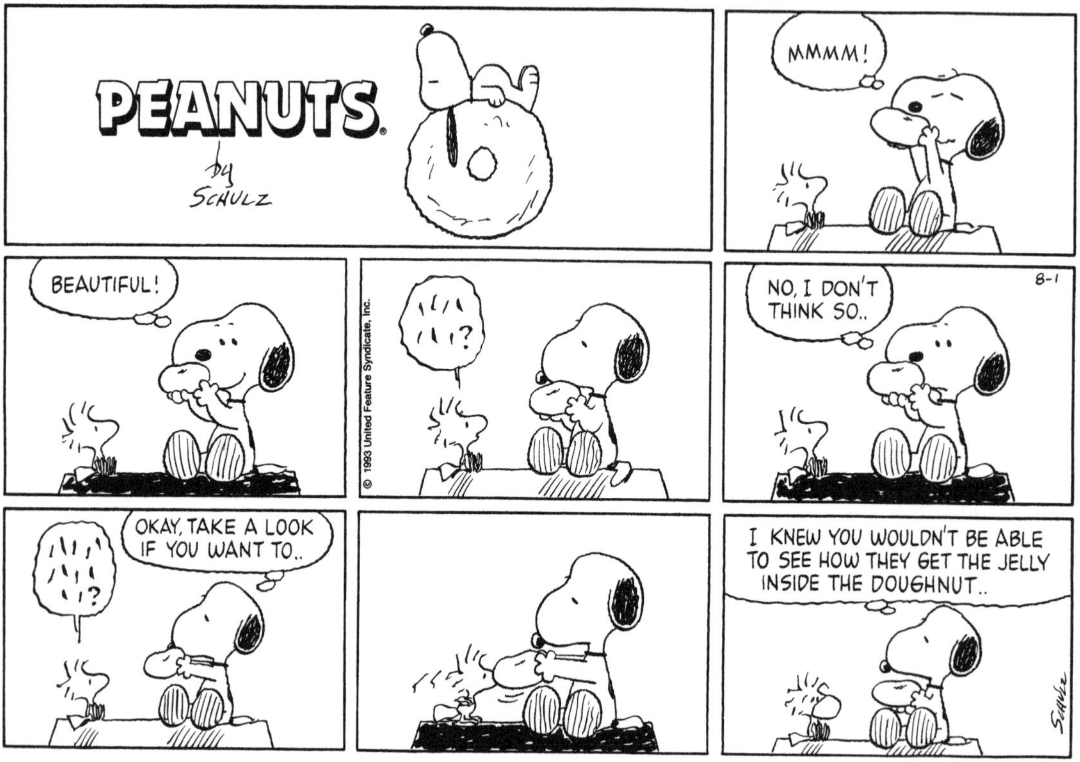
PEANUTS
by SCHULZ
MMMM!
BEAUTIFUL!
© 1993 United Feature Syndicate, Inc.
?
8-1
NO, I DON'T THINK SO..
?
OKAY, TAKE A LOOK IF YOU WANT TO..
I KNEW YOU WOULDN'T BE ABLE TO SEE HOW THEY GET THE JELLY INSIDE THE DOUGHNUT..
SCHULZ

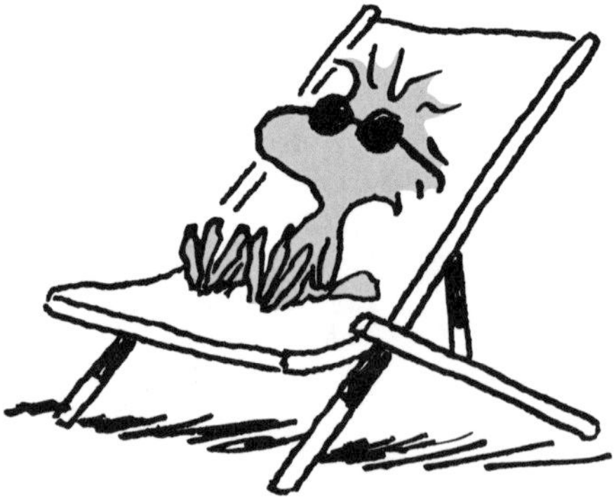

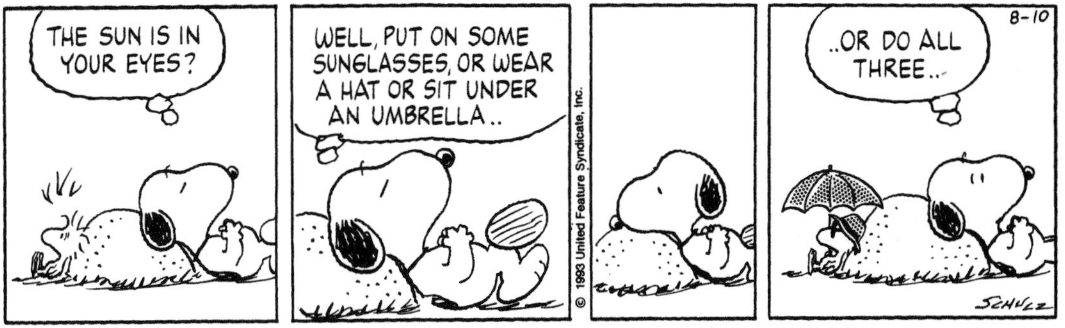
THE SUN IS IN YOUR EYES?
WELL, PUT ON SOME SUNGLASSES, OR WEAR A HAT OR SIT UNDER AN UMBRELLA..
© 1993 United Feature Syndicate, Inc.
8-10
..OR DO ALL THREE..
SCHULZ

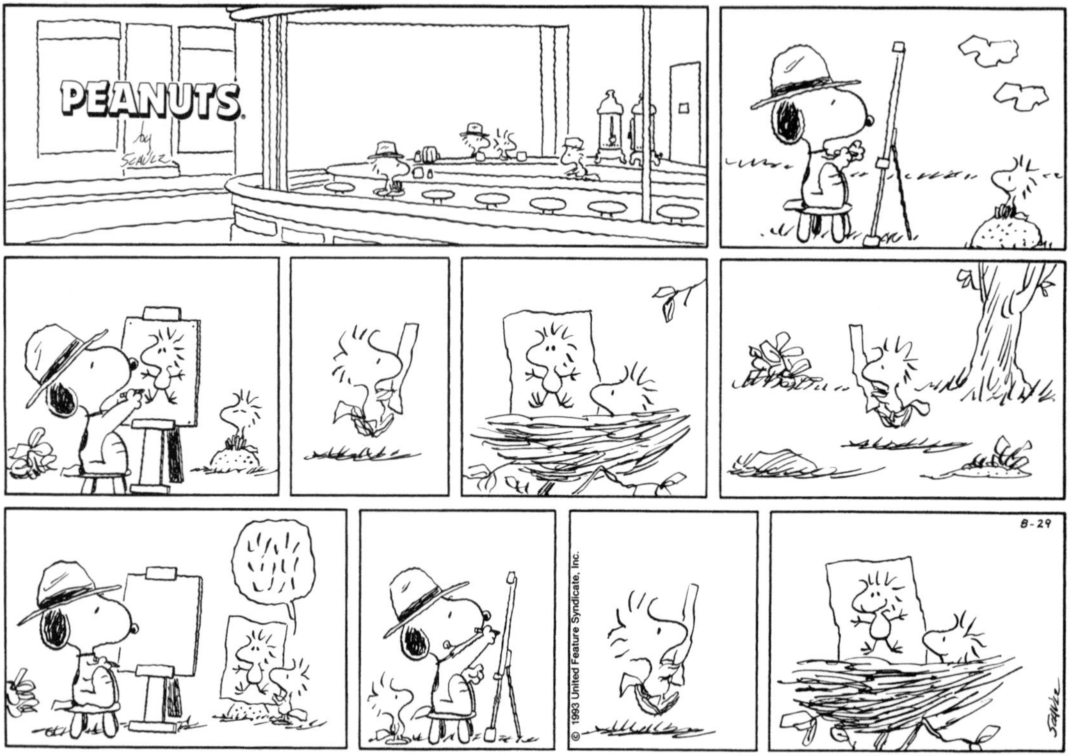
PEANUTS
by SCHULZ
8-29
© 1993 United Feature Syndicate, Inc.
SCHULZ

I'VE ALWAYS WONDERED WHY BIRDS FLY IN A "V" FORMATION...
YOUR MOM TOLD YOU TO ?
8-30
© 1993 United Feature Syndicate, Inc.
SCHULZ

10-4
© 1993 United Feature Syndicate, Inc.
PLEASE, YOU DON'T HAVE TO TELL ME EVERY LITTLE DETAIL!
SCHULZ

10-9

© 1993 United Feature Syndicate, Inc.

OKAY, GO LEAN
ON A CAT!

PEANUTS
by SCHULZ
THAT'S PERFECT!
WE'LL STAND BY THE DOOR, SEE, AND THEN YOU GO INTO YOUR ACT..
MAYBE WE'LL GET A LITTLE MIDDAY SNACK..
OKAY, GO TO IT..
2-27
© 1994 United Feature Syndicate, Inc.
DON'T FEEL BAD.. LOTS OF SHOWS CLOSE AFTER ONE PERFORMANCE..
SCHULZ

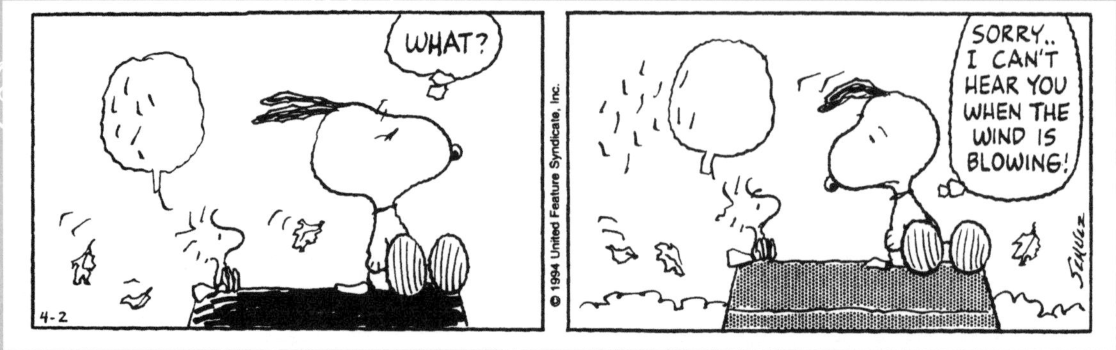
WHAT?
SORRY.. I CAN'T HEAR YOU WHEN THE WIND IS BLOWING!
4-2
© 1994 United Feature Syndicate, Inc.
SCHULZ

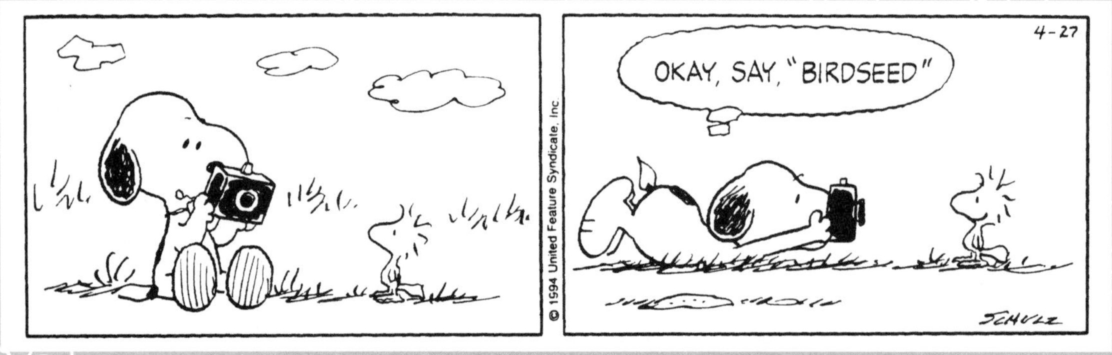
OKAY, SAY, "BIRDSEED"
4-27
© 1994 United Feature Syndicate, Inc.
SCHULZ

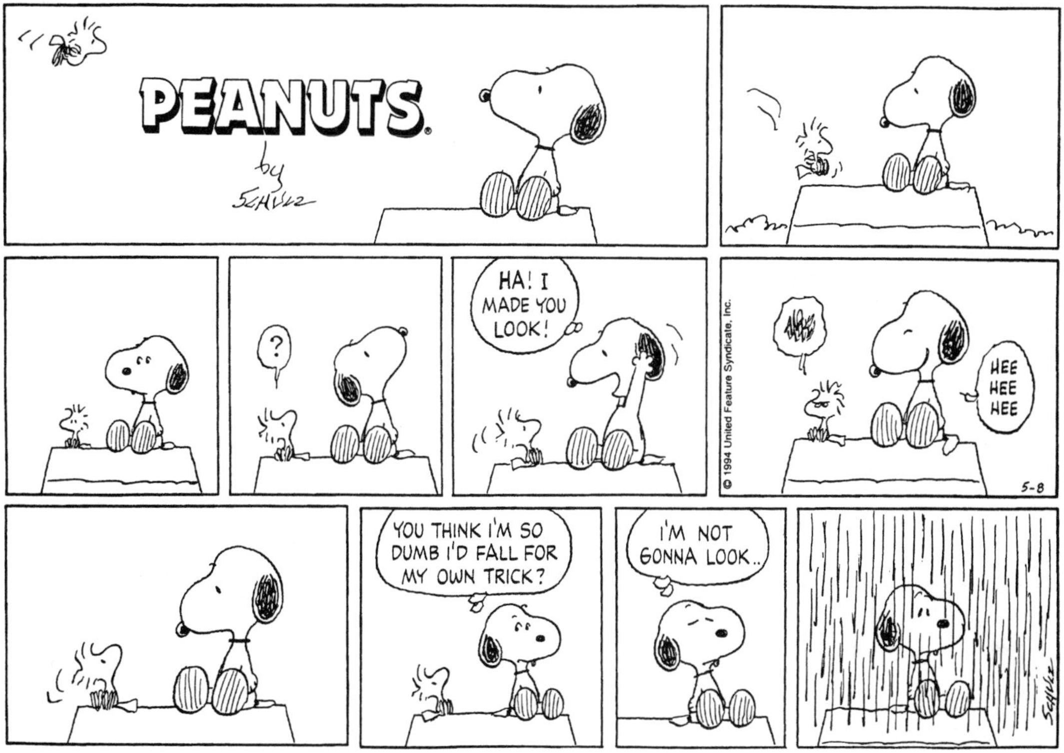
PEANUTS
by SCHULZ
HA! I MADE YOU LOOK!
HEE HEE HEE
YOU THINK I'M SO DUMB I'D FALL FOR MY OWN TRICK?
I'M NOT GONNA LOOK..
© 1994 United Feature Syndicate, Inc.
5-8

WOODSTOCK ALWAYS TELLS SUCH SAD STORIES..
SNIF
DOGS DON'T HAVE HANDKERCHIEFS
7-2
© 1994 United Feature Syndicate, Inc.
SCHULZ

YOU HAVE? YOU'VE ACTUALLY FLOWN ABOVE THE CLOUDS?
WOW! WHAT WAS IT LIKE?
WELL, YOU SHOULDN'T HAVE CLOSED YOUR EYES..
11-9
© 1994 United Feature Syndicate, Inc.
SCHULZ

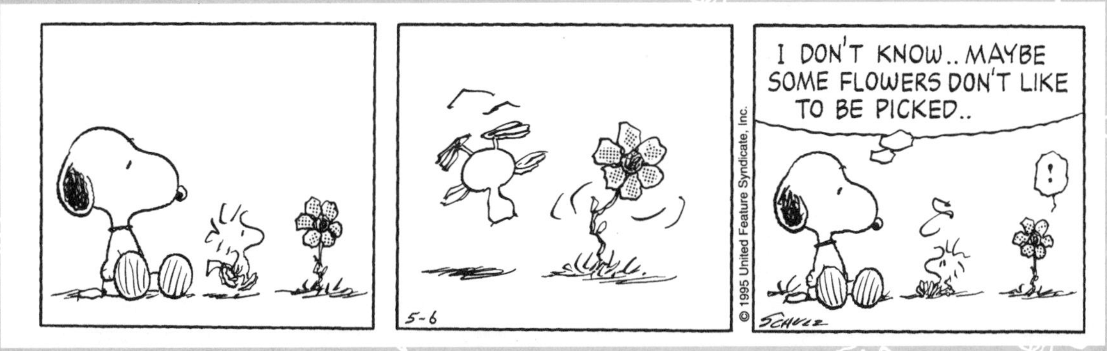
I DON'T KNOW.. MAYBE SOME FLOWERS DON'T LIKE TO BE PICKED..
!
5-6
© 1995 United Feature Syndicate, Inc.
SCHULZ

YES, I KNOW YOU DON'T LIKE TO BE CALLED "SHORTY"
AND I'VE NEVER CALLED YOU "SHORTY," HAVE I? NO, I HAVEN'T..
OF COURSE, YOU DON'T EXACTLY HAVE TO DUCK WHEN YOU GO THROUGH A DOOR, DO YOU?
boot!
5-22
© 1995 United Feature Syndicate, Inc.
SCHULZ

6-8
OKAY, YOU LOOK THERE, AND I'LL LOOK OVER HERE..
NO, I NEVER EVEN KNEW YOU WORE CONTACT LENSES..
© 1995 United Feature Syndicate, Inc.
SCHULZ

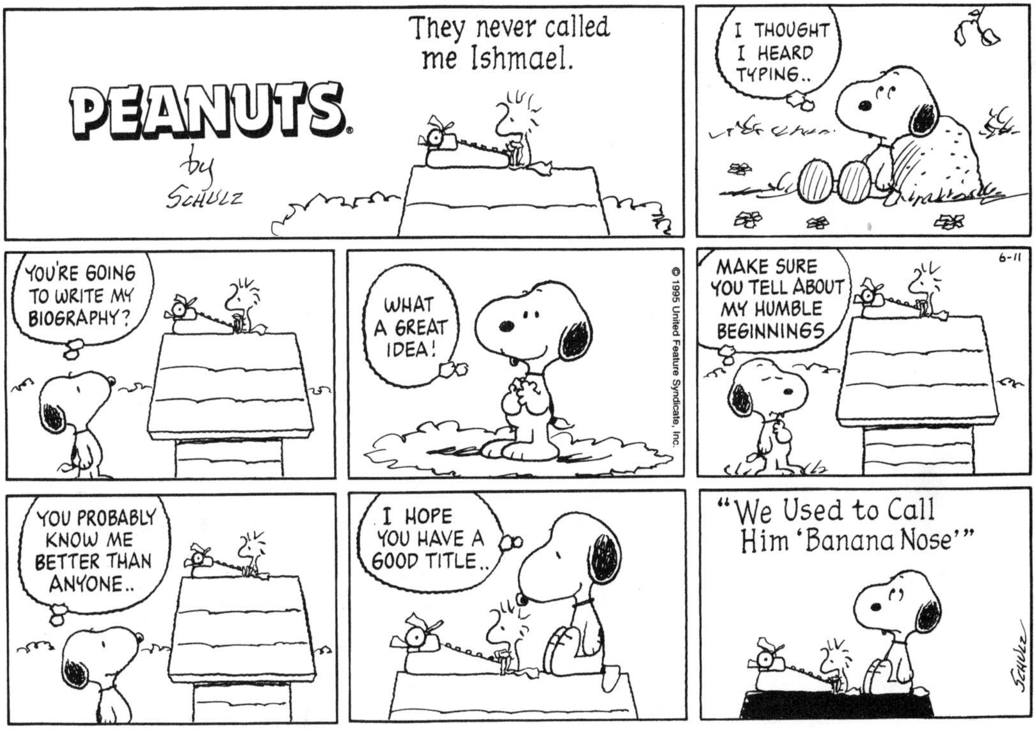
They never called me Ishmael.
PEANUTS.
by SCHULZ
I THOUGHT I HEARD TYPING..
YOU'RE GOING TO WRITE MY BIOGRAPHY?
WHAT A GREAT IDEA!
© 1995 United Feature Syndicate, Inc.
6-11
MAKE SURE YOU TELL ABOUT MY HUMBLE BEGINNINGS
YOU PROBABLY KNOW ME BETTER THAN ANYONE..
I HOPE YOU HAVE A GOOD TITLE..
"We Used to Call Him 'Banana Nose'"
SCHULZ

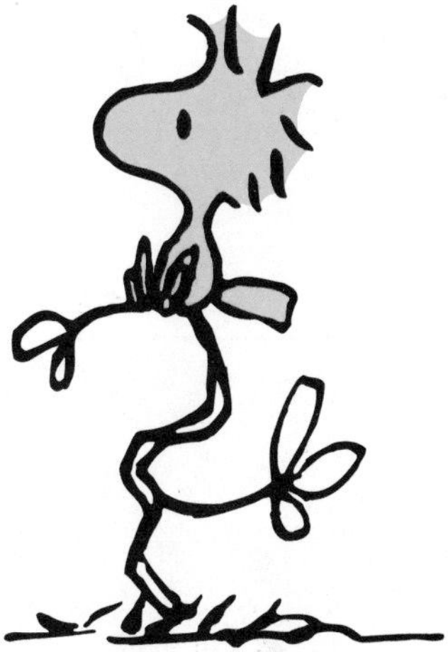

YOU'RE GOING TO THE MOON?
BUT YOU HAVE TO WEAR ONE OF THOSE THINGS ON YOUR HEAD..
WELL, YES... SORT OF LIKE THAT..
10-2
© 1995 United Feature Syndicate, Inc.
SCHULZ

SO YOU'RE REALLY GOING TO THE MOON..
I'M SURPRISED
I HOPE YOU REALIZE THAT WHEN YOU GET THERE, YOU'RE GOING TO BE ALL ALONE..
10-3
© 1995 United Feature Syndicate, Inc.
SCHULZ

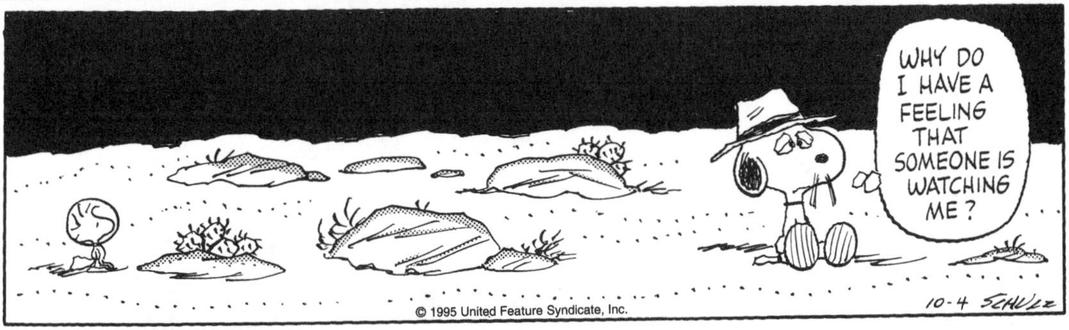
WHY DO I HAVE A FEELING THAT SOMEONE IS WATCHING ME ?
© 1995 United Feature Syndicate, Inc.
10-4 SCHULZ

IS THIS THE MOON?

SOMETIMES I WONDER..

HOW DID I GET HERE?

WELL, I LIKE TO THINK I CAME UP THE HARD WAY..

10-5

© 1995 United Feature Syndicate, Inc.

YES, WE'RE STANDING ON THE MOON, AND THAT'S THE EARTH WE'RE LOOKING AT..

BEFORE YOU GO BACK THERE'S SOMETHING OVER HERE YOU SHOULDN'T MISS..

MOON ROCKS FOR SALE

10-6

© 1995 United Feature Syndicate, Inc.

YOU'RE BACK FROM THE MOON? WOW! WHAT AN ADVENTURE! TELL ME WHAT YOU SAW

A WEIRD CREATURE? LET'S SEE THE PICTURE..

THAT'S MY BROTHER SPIKE! MY FAVORITE BROTHER! GOOD OL' WONDERFUL SPIKE

© 1995 United Feature Syndicate, Inc.

10-7

HE SOLD YOU A MOON ROCK?

WHAT I DON'T UNDERSTAND IS HOW YOU CAN FLY AROUND UP THERE WITHOUT BUMPING INTO ANOTHER BIRD..

12-27

© 1995 United Feature Syndicate, Inc.

NO, I REALIZE YOU'RE NOT STUPID..

LISTEN TO THOSE GEESE FLYING OVER.."HONK, HONK, HONK, HONK"
THEY KEEP SAYING THE SAME THING OVER AND OVER.."HONK, HONK, HONK, HONK.."
NO, I DON'T EXPECT THE GETTYSBURG ADDRESS..
12-28
© 1995 United Feature Syndicate, Inc.
SCHULZ

SOMETIMES THE BIRD DUNKS THE DOUGHNUT..
SOMETIMES THE DOUGHNUT DUNKS THE BIRD..
4-29
© 1996 United Feature Syndicate, Inc.
SCHULZ

NO, I DON'T HAVE A BATHMAT..

© 1996 United Feature Syndicate, Inc.

NO, I HAVEN'T SEEN YOUR MOM

I DON'T EVEN KNOW WHAT SHE LOOKS LIKE.. DOES SHE HAVE A NAME?

6-15

© 1996 United Feature Syndicate, Inc.

BUT I IMAGINE A LOT OF THEM ARE CALLED "BIRD MOM"

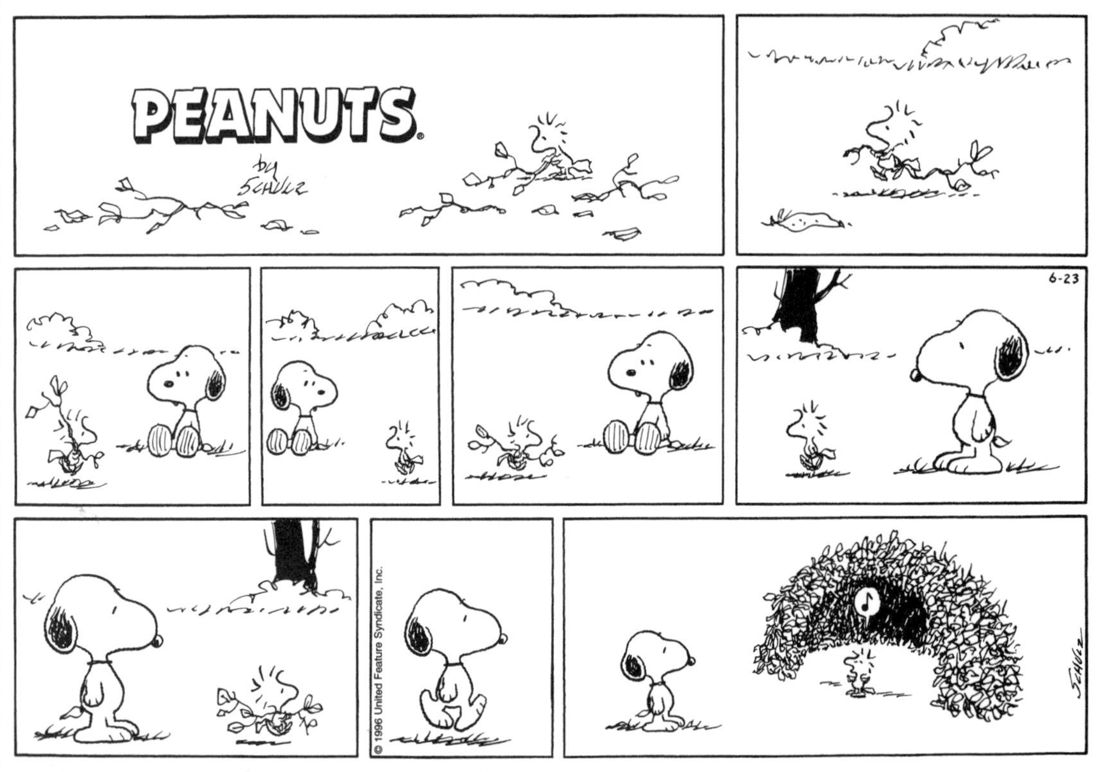
PEANUTS®
by SCHULZ
6-23
© 1996 United Feature Syndicate, Inc.
SCHULZ

THERE'S A BUNCH OF BIRD WATCHERS OUT TODAY..
www.unitedmedia.com
THEY'LL BE TAKING PICTURES SO YOU SHOULD GET OUT AND START FLYING AROUND..
9-27
© 1996 United Feature Syndicate, Inc.
THAT'S NOT EXACTLY WHAT I MEANT..
SCHULZ

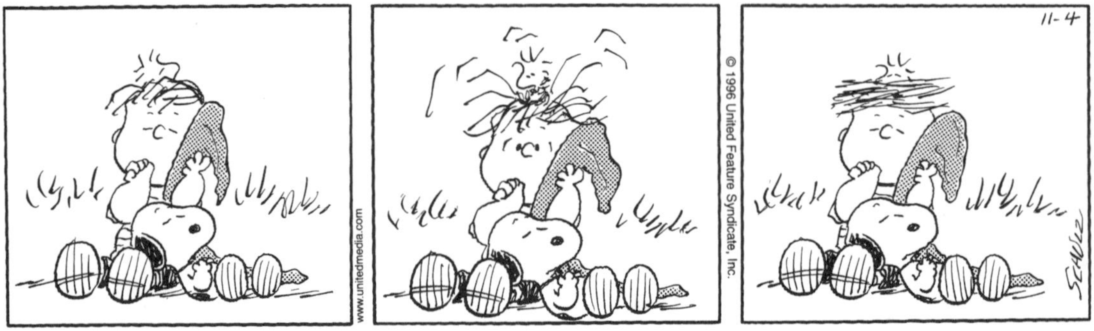
11-4
© 1996 United Feature Syndicate, Inc.
www.unitedmedia.com
SCHULZ

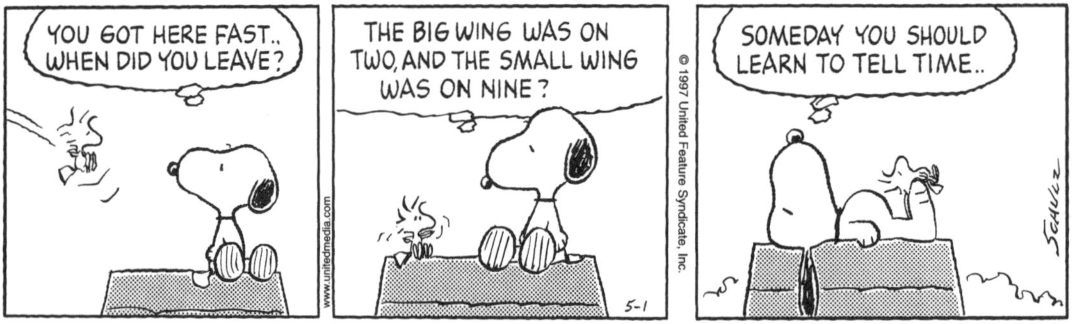
YOU GOT HERE FAST.. WHEN DID YOU LEAVE?
THE BIG WING WAS ON TWO, AND THE SMALL WING WAS ON NINE?
SOMEDAY YOU SHOULD LEARN TO TELL TIME..
5-1
© 1997 United Feature Syndicate, Inc.
www.unitedmedia.com
SCHULZ

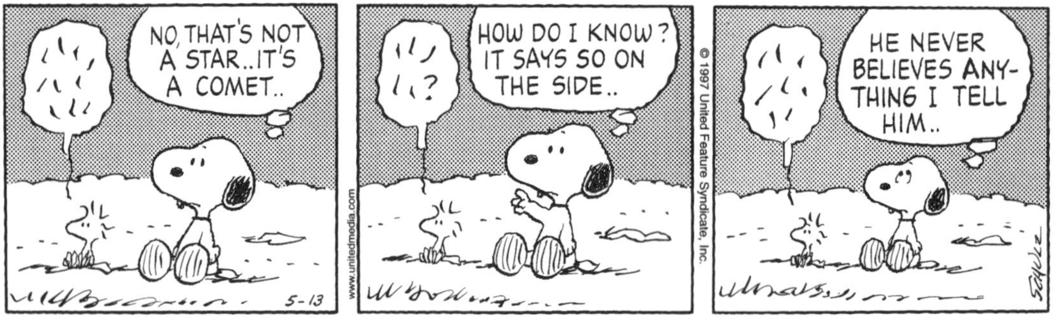
NO, THAT'S NOT A STAR..IT'S A COMET..
HOW DO I KNOW? IT SAYS SO ON THE SIDE..
HE NEVER BELIEVES ANYTHING I TELL HIM..
5-13
© 1997 United Feature Syndicate, Inc.
www.unitedmedia.com
SCHULZ

I'VE OFTEN WONDERED IF YOU CAN SEE THE OCEAN FROM THERE..
7-5
© 1997 United Feature Syndicate, Inc.
NO? THEN I THINK YOU CAN TAKE THE LIFE JACKET OFF..
SCHULZ

IF I GET A BITE, YOU GRAB THE NET..
www.unitedmedia.com
NOW!
8-16
© 1997 United Feature Syndicate, Inc.
SCHULZ

HE HAS THESE REINDEER, SEE, AND THEY FLY THROUGH THE AIR PULLING HIS SLED...
AND IF YOU BELIEVE THAT, I HAVE A GOLD BIRD NEST THAT I'LL SELL YOU FOR A DOLLAR!
HAHAHAHAHA!
MERRY CHRISTMAS, LITTLE FRIEND..
12-24-97
SCHULZ
© 1987 United Feature Syndicate, Inc.

IT'S TOO BAD YOU'RE NOT A HAWK..
SOME PEOPLE BELIEVE THAT HAWKS HAVE "ACCESS TO THE HEAVENS"
WELL, YES.. ACCESS TO THE MALL IS PRETTY GOOD..
www.unitedmedia.com
© 1998 United Feature Syndicate, Inc.
1-29
SCHULZ

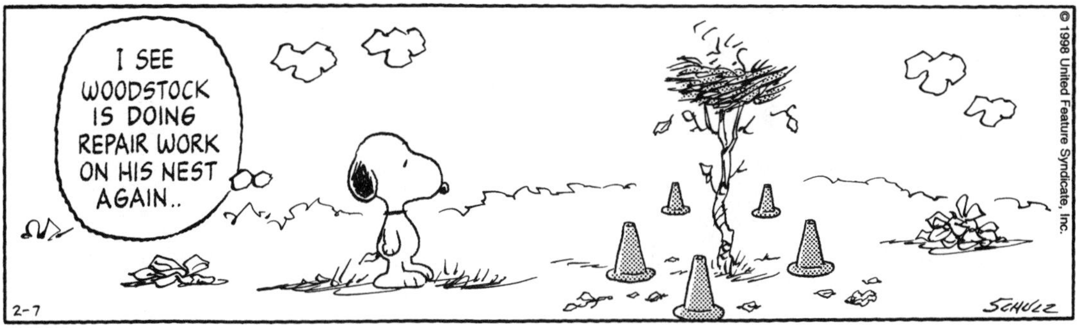
I SEE WOODSTOCK IS DOING REPAIR WORK ON HIS NEST AGAIN..
2-7
SCHULZ
© 1998 United Feature Syndicate, Inc.

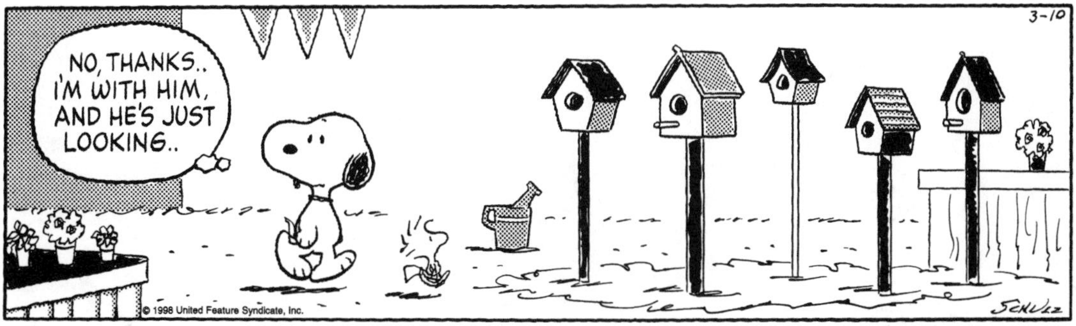
NO, THANKS.. I'M WITH HIM, AND HE'S JUST LOOKING..
3-10
SCHULZ
© 1998 United Feature Syndicate, Inc.

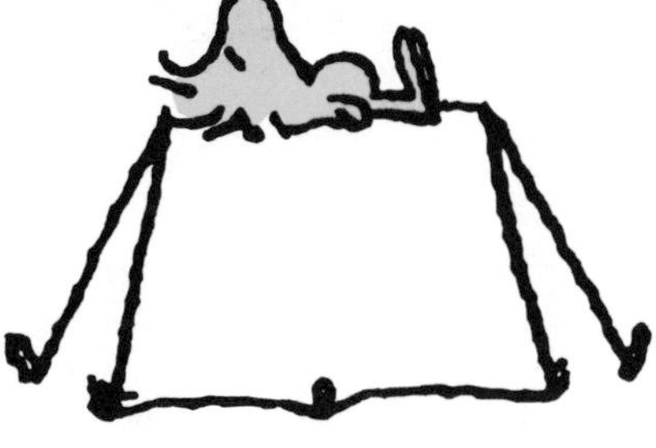

4-28
© 1998 United Feature Syndicate, Inc.
YES, THAT'S BETTER..NOW YOU LOOK VERY WEALTHY..
SCHULZ

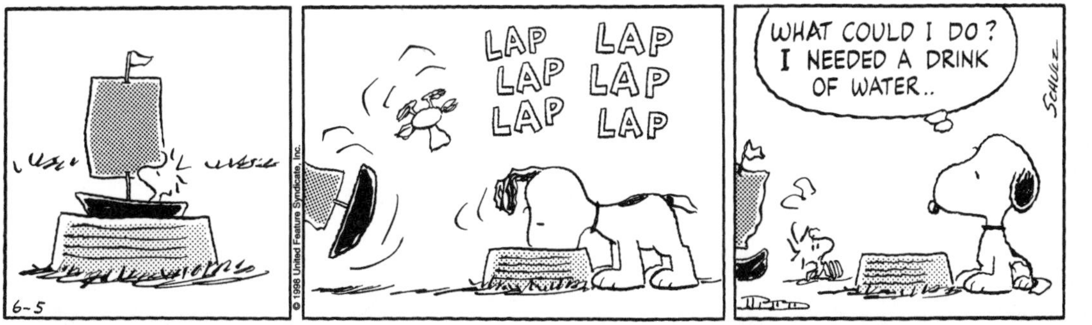
6-5
© 1998 United Feature Syndicate, Inc.
LAP LAP
LAP LAP
LAP LAP
WHAT COULD I DO? I NEEDED A DRINK OF WATER..
SCHULZ

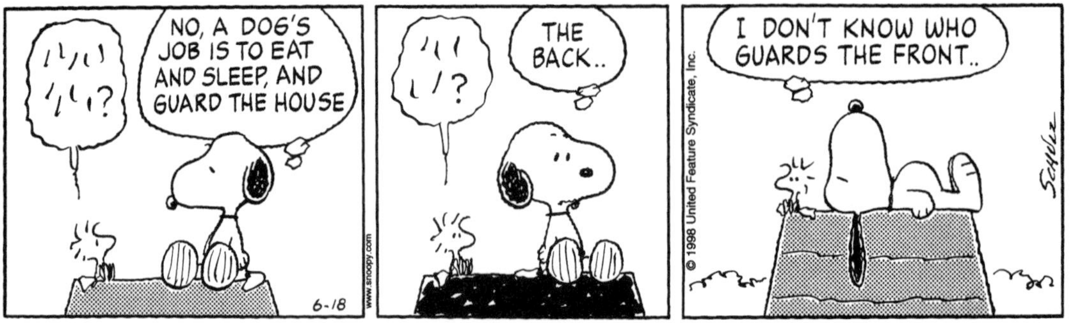
NO, A DOG'S JOB IS TO EAT AND SLEEP, AND GUARD THE HOUSE
6-18
www.snoopy.com
THE BACK..
© 1998 United Feature Syndicate, Inc.
I DON'T KNOW WHO GUARDS THE FRONT..
SCHULZ

I AGREE.. STUPID TREE!
© 1998 United Feature Syndicate, Inc.
www.snoopy.com
SCHULZ
6-19

DOG FOOD? WELL, IT USUALLY HAS A HEARTY FLAVOR..A LITTLE SPICY..MAYBE A TOUCH OF GAMINESS...
6-27
© 1998 United Feature Syndicate, Inc.
www.snoopy.com
NO, I DON'T WANT TO KNOW WHAT A WORM TASTES LIKE..
SCHULZ

THE FIRST THING YOU DO IS RAISE YOUR GLASS..
THEN YOU SAY, "I'LL DRINK TO THAT!"
8-12
© 1998 United Feature Syndicate, Inc.
IT TAKES A LITTLE PRACTICE..
SCHULZ

© 1998 United Feature Syndicate, Inc.
www.snoopy.com
11-4
I DON'T KNOW..HOW CAN YOU GET YOUR FOOT CAUGHT IN A NEST ?
SCHULZ

NO, I'M NOT INTERESTED..
2-20
www.snoopy.com
NO, NOT TODAY, THANK YOU..
© 1999 United Feature Syndicate, Inc.
NO, BUT WHY DON'T YOU JUST LEAVE ME YOUR CARD ?
SALESBIRDS !
SCHULZ

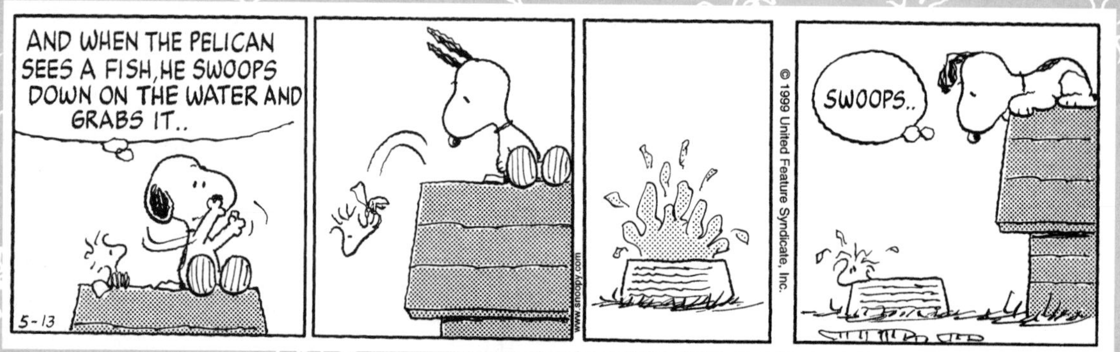
AND WHEN THE PELICAN SEES A FISH, HE SWOOPS DOWN ON THE WATER AND GRABS IT..
5-13
www.snoopy.com
© 1999 United Feature Syndicate, Inc.
SWOOPS..

KEEP LOOKING UP..THAT'S THE SECRET OF LIFE...
5-29
www.snoopy.com
KLUNK!
© 1999 United Feature Syndicate, Inc.
I WAS WRONG.. THAT'S NOT THE SECRET OF LIFE..

AND THEN THE POET SAID, "WHAT IS SO RARE AS A DAY IN JUNE?"
6-5
www.snoopy.com
WHICH DAY? I DON'T KNOW WHICH DAY.. WHO CARES?
© 1999 United Feature Syndicate, Inc.
YOU DIDN'T LIKE YESTERDAY?
SCHULZ

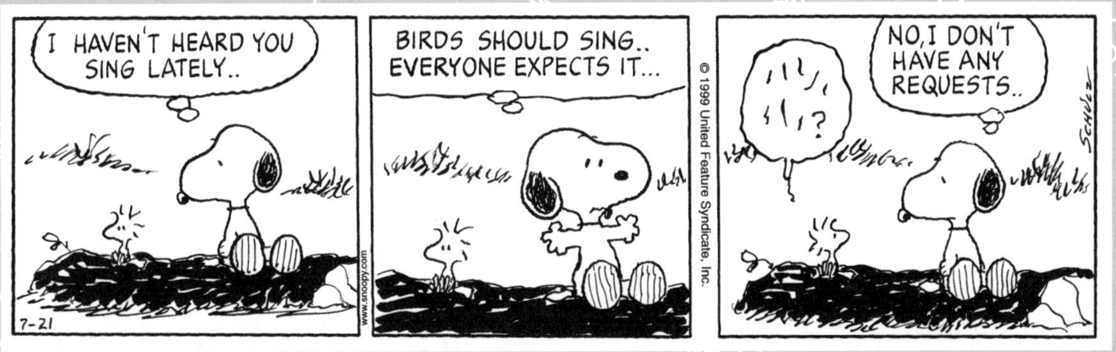
I HAVEN'T HEARD YOU SING LATELY..
7-21
www.snoopy.com
BIRDS SHOULD SING.. EVERYONE EXPECTS IT...
© 1999 United Feature Syndicate, Inc.
NO, I DON'T HAVE ANY REQUESTS..
SCHULZ

10-26
www.snoopy.com
© 1999 United Feature Syndicate, Inc.
"RETURN TO SENDER"
SCHULZ

SO AFTER YOU BUILT YOUR NEST IN THIS TREE, THE TREE FELL DOWN..
12-29
www.snoopy.com
© 1999 United Feature Syndicate, Inc.
SO AFTER YOU BUILT YOUR NEST IN THIS TREE, THE TREE FELL DOWN..
SCHULZ

PEANUTS
BIRDS HAVE SOME PECULIAR ATTRIBUTES...
1-15
WHEN BIRDS FALL ASLEEP ON TREE BRANCHES, THEIR CLAWS AUTOMATICALLY TIGHTEN TO KEEP THEM FROM FALLING OFF...
WHICH CAN BE VERY HARD ON THE BRANCHES...
Tm. Reg. U.S. Pat. Off.—All rights reserved ©1974 by United Feature Syndicate, Inc.
OR SOMEONE'S NOSE!
SCHULZ

PEANUTS
WOODSTOCK SURE SEEMS TO BE RESTLESS...
ALL THAT TOSSING AND TURNING...
1-26
NOW ON HIS BACK, NOW ON HIS STOMACH, NOW ON HIS SIDE...
Tm. Reg. U.S. Pat. Off.—All rights reserved ©1974 by United Feature Syndicate, Inc.
HE LOOKS LIKE HE'S BEING BASTED!
SCHULZ

PEANUTS
I KIND OF ENVY WOODSTOCK..
Z
HE DOESN'T SEEM TO HAVE TOO MANY ANXIETIES...
Z
1-17
Tm Reg. U.S. Pat. Off.—All rights reserved ©1974 by United Feature Syndicate Inc.
JUST A BAD DREAM NOW AND THEN..
Z
SCHULZ